Your Towns and Cities in tl

Coventry
in the Great War

Dedication

For Two True Sky Blues
Christopher and Anita McKeogh

Your Towns and Cities in the Great War

Coventry
in the Great War

Leonard Markham

Pen & Sword
MILITARY

First published in Great Britain in 2014 by
PEN & SWORD MILITARY
an imprint of
Pen and Sword Books Ltd
47 Church Street
Barnsley
South Yorkshire S70 2AS

ISBN 978 1 78346 397 8

Printed and bound in England
by Page Bros, Norwich

Typeset in Times New Roman by Chic Graphics

Pen & Sword Books Ltd incorporates the imprints of
Pen & Sword Archaeology, Atlas, Aviation, Battleground, Discovery,
Family History, History, Maritime, Military, Naval, Politics, Railways,
Select, Social History, Transport, True Crime, Claymore Press,
Frontline Books, Leo Cooper, Praetorian Press, Remember When,
Seaforth Publishing and Wharncliffe.

For a complete list of Pen and Sword titles please contact
Pen and Sword Books Limited
47 Church Street, Barnsley, South Yorkshire, S70 2AS, England
E-mail: enquiries@pen-and-sword.co.uk
Website: www.pen-and-sword.co.uk

Printed and bound in England

Contents

Pack up your troubles in your old kit bag,
And smile, smile, smile,
While you've a lucifer to light your fag,
Smile boys that's the style.

Refrain of the men of Coventry
as they turned their backs on the three spires
and marched off to war.

Eighteenth century etching of Coventry panorama.
(Leonard Markham Archive)

'I waited for the train at Coventry,
I hung with grooms and porters on the bridge,
To watch the three tall spires; and there I shaped,
The city's ancient legend into this…'

The first four lines of Tennyson's poem *Godiva* written in 1840

Preface by the Author

At the time of the commissioning of this work, I knew very little about Coventry and its people. As a recently arrived resident of Kenilworth, I had an overriding, false impression of the great metropolis on my doorstep as a workaday place, famous only for the legend of Lady Godiva. Having only casually visited Coventry, my initial impressions were of a city still haunted by the terrible events of two world wars, its fortunes further depressed by the changing global nature of industry and the scourge of unemployment. But then I took to the streets on foot, talked to its residents and opened its ancient books, casting a searchlight on a more accurate reality, realising that the Coventry bedrock is over a thousand years of monastic and spiritual history. I found ingenuity, invention, enterprise, hard work and dedication, stoicism in adversity and an abiding capacity for adaptation, many generations of newcomers from across the globe adding verve and colour to an international beacon city that in its modern aspirations leads the world in fostering peace and reconciliation.

Any newcomer to this city on the hill naturally wanders to the gaunt eminence dominated by the ruins of Coventry Cathedral. Everybody should go there and go there they must. Not to weep or be melancholy at the death and destruction wrought by the Luftwaffe on that fateful night in 1940 but to be inspired. For that ruin has been and perennially is a springboard for renewal. Its remarkable energy flows into the soaring rafters of the replacement cathedral next door, spreading out to the nearby council chamber, the university, the commercial precincts and beyond. This soul of Coventry – the world's first 'Twin City', linked with Stalingrad during the Second World War and Hiroshima shortly afterwards - helps define the town, and its noble purpose reflected in its designation as a City of Peace and Reconciliation and the establishment of a Centre for the Study of Forgiveness at the university in 2000.

This book tells the necessarily abridged but unadorned story of Coventry during the Great War of 1914-18. The mood in those desperate years changed from one of jingoistic excitement at the outset to one of dour resignation, degenerating into sunken-eyed melancholia and bitterness at the end. These moods were reflected in the sentiments of the popular songs of the period and I have used the titles and lyrics of some of these as my chapter headings

My ancestors fought in the Great War but, two generations on, my knowledge of the conflict has been vague and sketchy ... until now. The book is largely a record of triumph in adversity but some of the descriptions of the lives of both combatants and civilians are upsetting. Unapologetically, I retell the stories of these Coventrians faithfully and without embellishment so that readers can, in some small way, get a whiff of the odour of fear and despair both at home and on the battlefield. Amidst all the mayhem and carnage, the story I found the most shocking and abhorrent of all was that of Private Albert Troughton, who was executed in April 1915. His death is described currently by the Shot at Dawn Campaign, who seek pardons for the 306 men who were despatched by firing squad during the war, as: 'Judicial murder. They were brutally gunned down not in the name of justice but as a stupid, spiteful and shameful example to others.'

The plethora of archival material available would sink a dreadnought so I have had to be selective. My aim has been to try to give varied snapshots of ordinary lives, working conditions and events, detailing the fears, hopes, dreams and tragedies of home life in the city, interspersed with a juxtaposed but limited selection of relevant military narratives from across the world to give a wider perspective and balance and to give a feel for the international events that touched the lives of Coventry people.

In this centenary year of 2014, I hope I have been successful.

Leonard Markham
Kenilworth
2014

Note: Headings under the Three Spires logo spotlight varied aspects of domestic life in the city – the Royal Warwickshire Regiment logo introduces relevant military material.

Introduction

Harry Patch, 'The Last Surviving Tommy' died, aged 111, at a Somerset nursing home in 2009, his demise bringing to a close the fighting man's memory of the Great War. In this centenary year of 2014 there are still alive a very small number of other centenarians who witnessed the outbreak of the conflict as young children but soon they, too, will be gone, leaving the events of 1914-18 to our ancestors and the historians. Many books and pamphlets have been written about the contributions and sacrifices service men and women from Coventry made to the war effort. For now, we will not add to their number, although one hundred years on, it seems wholly appropriate to remember and honour in a commemorative book the civilians of this great city who invested so much of their labours and skills, energies and ultimately lives in supporting the monumental struggle with Germany and her allies.

Prelude to
War and Beginnings

The annexation of the French provinces of Alsace and Lorraine after a rousing victory in the Franco – Prussian War of 1870/71, helped inspire the creation in 1871 of a new German state with pan-European ambitions and a plan to compete with Great Britain for naval supremacy. Driven by a new sense of identity and superiority, by enterprise and freely available credit that stimulated innovation and expansion, its population increased from 41 million to 65.3 million in just four decades. Before long, dreadnoughts were regularly gliding down the slips of Kiel and Wilhelmshaven and by 1914, fledgling Germany was an economic powerhouse and the most populous nation west of Russia with an army of four million regulars and conscripted men. A third as big again as Great Britain, it was a nation flexing its expansionist muscles with an historic grudge against the world that was fanned into a furnace of hatred by successive German statesmen, diplomats and merchants. And it, and its allies – Austria-Hungary, Bulgaria and the Ottoman Empire - looked west across the German Ocean and east to Russia and its satellites with contempt and envy.

The German appetite for war had long been festering. On 9 November 1911, August Bebel, a German Marxist politician – one of the founders of the Social Democratic Party – addressed the Reichstag. 'There will be a catastrophe,' he warned. 'Sixteen to eighteen million men, the flower of different nations, will march against each other equipped with lethal weapons. I am convinced that this great march will be followed by a great collapse,' (laughter and derision). 'All right, you have laughed about it, but it will come. What will be the result? After this war, we will have mass bankruptcy, mass misery, mass unemployment and great famine.'

But nobody listened to Herr Bebel, even the Association of German Jews proclaiming that every German Jew was 'ready to sacrifice all the property and blood demanded by duty'.

The sounds of war in Great Britain were at first muted but month on month the drumsticks beat louder, the national mood changing to one of expectancy, resolution and inevitability, the country and its empire preparing both nationally and locally. In Coventry, even school children caught the martial strains, permission being granted to establish a Cadet Corps at the distinguished Bablake School as early as 1912. Just one year later, the school had its own rifle range. Manufacturing firms in the city gradually expanded, built bigger premises, took on more workers and re-tooled, the famous White and Poppe Ltd, which had been established in Drake Street in 1899 to make single cylinder, water-cooled motor engines, taking on lucrative contracts to supply fuse bodies for high explosive shells. A few days after the first shots were fired in France, its reputation for excellence and reliability in delivering orders during the Boer War (1899-1902), earned it an order for 10,000 aluminium fuses and 10,000 brass 18-pounder shell-sockets per week. Within a few weeks, its managing director, Reginald Bacon, spent almost the entire day taking orders on the telephone and as orders increased he quickly oversaw the erection of new workshops. Eventually, his firm's output would include 710 aircraft, 111 tanks, 92 anti-aircraft guns, nearly 400,000 cartridge cases and millions of fuses and detonators. Coventry was becoming an arsenal, all manner of people from all over the United Kingdom flocking to the city attracted by job prospects and high wages. Female hands at White and Poppe were more visible than most, their constant shell filling with highly explosive powders causing a distinctive yellowing of the skin. Some of these blue-overalled and mob-capped 'Canaries' or 'Tetrol Girls' flaunted their unheard of earning power by buying luxurious fur coats, the apparent wealth of the city attracting yet more newcomers.

Such was the clamour for accommodation that improvised housing had to be quickly erected within commuting distance of the factories. The single storey Munitions Cottages in Foleshill were typical of the period, with their breezeblock construction and roofs constructed of fabric-covered wood.

Alfred Herbert headed another company heavily committed to producing war materials, summing up the fevered mood in the city in the following words:

> 'The effect of the war on the engineering industry has been to render demand, enormously and continuously, in excess of supply. It has not been a question of obtaining orders, but, on the contrary, every engineering concern has been swamped with orders in excess of its possible output and competition, for the time being, has ceased to exist.'

'Never was a hammer allowed to stand idle!' remarked an exhausted employee of Thomas Smith's Stamping Works in Red Lane. 'If a stamper was sick, or for any reason couldn't come to work, his hammer **had** to be kept going. Many a time, I can remember, after I'd done a hard day's work and gone home, there came a knock at the door. This was the foreman on the night-shift come over from the stamp shop to ask me to take another man's place on the hammer. I swallowed my tea and back I went; but many of us did it often.'

CHAPTER 1

1914:
Your King and Country Need You

Have you seen the Royal Proclamation?
Caused by war's alarms.
Words addressed to all the population,
Calling us to arms!

Not for mad ambitions greed England asks us in her need,
To face the foeman's guns,
'Tis honour, truth and right,
For glorious liberty we fight,
To crush the envious foeman's might,
That England wants her sons!

Come on Tommy – come on Jack,
We'll guard the home till you come back.
Come on Sandy, come on Pat for you're true blue!
Down your tools and leave your benches,
Say goodbye to all the wenches,
Take up your gun and may God speed you,
For your King and Country need you!

The tipping point in the delicate European balance of power was reached on 28 June 1914, when the heir to the Austrian and Hungarian thrones and his wife were assassinated by a Serbian terrorist during an official visit to Sarajevo, capital of the newly annexed province of Bosnia. Austria-Hungary saw an opportunity to crush Serbia and assert its authority in the Balkans and sought German approval to a very stiff ultimatum against its neighbour. Germany, in turn, perceived a golden opportunity of becoming the leading power in Europe, of knocking Great Britain off its imperial perch and achieving world status. At a stroke, its bold ambition was to split and overwhelm its rivals, baulk Russian modernization, eradicate dangers to Austria-Hungary and sideline domestic opposition. The threats and diplomatic rhetoric led to mass mobilizations and ultimatums and on 1 August Germany declared war on Russia and then on France two days later, German troops invading little Belgium with 760,000 men on 4 August. Under the terms of an 1839 treaty, Britain, amongst others, had guaranteed Belgian independence and neutrality, its legal obligations and the obvious threat to the balance of power and the Channel ports leading to an inevitable decision. At 11 pm on 4 August 1914, Britain declared war on Germany.

The declaration had been anticipated by an excited and jingoistic population reared on the notion that imperialist Britain had brought universal civilization, liberty and culture to the world, every schoolchild in the country waving the Union Jack over a world atlas that showed a rash of imperial pink on every continent. With God's help, Britain was ready to protect its empire, the idea that it had a deeply moral duty – A RIGHT OVER MIGHT – to defend the causes of freedom and justice, inspiring every citizen to applaud the announcement.

FULL OF FEAR AND TREMBLING

'When I was quite young, I was taken by my father to hear Lord Roberts at the Coventry Drill Hall. He made a speech which I was too young to understand thoroughly, but in which he spoke of the danger confronting England and the need for conscription. I was then imbued with a great fear that I should called upon to be a soldier. A year or two later, sketch maps appeared in the daily papers showing where Germany was going to place mines and blow up this and that. At the age of 14 or 15, I was full of fear and trembling that I might have to become a soldier sooner or later! I did not want to become a wartime soldier. I always wanted to be an army bandmaster.

When I was 17, hostilities between England and Germany began and I could see that my prospects of becoming a bandmaster were to be squashed, at least for the time being. My father and mother, who were both very patriotic people, spoke to me seriously on the question of whether or not I should join the army. They emphatically stated that they would do everything in their power to prevent me giving a false age and joining the ranks before I had attained the age of 19.'

(Recollections of Eric Jordan of Humber Avenue, Coventry. A well-known pianist and entertainer after the war, Eric was the secretary of the Coventry Musical Club.)

FOOTBALL FORTUNES

Rumblings of war were not allowed to blow the whistle on an Englishman's favourite recreation, the final of the charity fundraising Coventry Nursing Cup taking place between Foleshill Albions and Rugby at the end of a long season. Albion skipper, Jephcote, was presented with the famous 41 inches high trophy after his team beat a spirited opposition 3-2. With a capacity of 4½ gallons, the cup held enough amber liquid for toasts by all the winning players - plus substitutes. The cup continued to be drained throughout the conflict. The winners in subsequent seasons were Newdigate Colliery, Coventry Ordnance, Standard Works and Daimler Athletic.

The fortunes of professional football club Coventry City were not so rosy. As the nation lurched into war, a sizeable contingent of the squad left for France, the club recording an annual loss of £1500 with further debts accruing of £200. On top of that, they were summonsed for not paying rates! After the last match in 1915 it would be a further three years before a ball would be kicked, although CFC remained an entity with rent and expenses to pay. Still struggling with annual losses of £500 per year, the club reached its nadir in 1917 and faced extinction. Enter benefactor David Cooke – he made his money as a tobacconist, introducing his noted *Three Cups* brand in 1891 – who paid off three and a half years' back rent on the Highfield Road ground, becoming its sole tenant until his death in 1932.

Tragically, Coventry City FC players John Tosswill, Alf Edwards, Stephen Jackson, Jack Hankins, Tom Morris, Walter Kimberley, Mick

Hanson and George Warden would never again pull on the famous shirt.

In an article published soon after the war began, the *Coventry Herald* noted: 'The professional footballer is no longer a public idol. When the war is over and football resumes, one expects to see Coventry Rugby Club once again the most popular club as in the olden days and Coventry a distinctly rugby town.'

EXCITED CHEERS AT THE DECLARATION OF WAR

'News reached milling crowds in Coventry at midnight on Tuesday. The masses cheered excitedly and began singing patriotic songs including *Rule Britannia* and *Three Cheers for the Red, White and Blue.*' (*Coventry Telegraph.*)

There were tumultuous scenes across the nation, the actress Tilla Durieux proclaiming: 'Every face looks happy. We've got war! One's food gets cold. One's beer gets warm. No matter – we've got war!'

Within a few days, an appeal was printed in the *Coventry Graphic:*

YOUR KING & COUNTRY NEED YOU
A CALL TO ARMS
An addition of 100,000 men to his
Majesty's regular Army is immediately
necessary in the present grave National emergency.
Lord Kitchener is confident that this appeal
will be at once responded to by all those who
have the safety of our Empire at heart.

TERMS OF SERVICE
General service for a period of three years
or until the war is concluded.

HOW TO JOIN
Full information can be obtained
at any post office in the Kingdom, or at
any military depot.

GOD SAVE THE KING!

This appeal, backed up by many in the clergy who championed the concept of 'Muscular Christianity' – a doctrine that gave divine backing to the killing of Germans - had eager and beaming young men queuing to sign up for a war that was confidently predicted to be concluded by Christmas. Such appeals were meet with fervour despite the fact that no British soldier had fired a shot in anger in western Europe since the last salvo on the battlefield of Waterloo some ninety-nine years earlier. Recruits had the gun smoke of Wellington and Nelson in their nostrils, although one Coventry stalwart was deflated by the bureaucracy and the hot sun, lamenting: 'I have waited six hours this week trying to get into the army. Such delay does not encourage one's patriotism.'

BUGGER DE KAISER!
Patriotic fervour brought terror to a Coventry neighbourhood even before the ink on the recruitment forms was dry. Even in 1914, the city was a multi-cultural centre. One incomer, who had lived here for some years, did not share the appetite for war. Rudolph Henniger, former head waiter at the *King's Head* in Hertford Street, prospered and invested in a small tobacconist's shop at the corner of Charterhouse Road and Northfield Road. Jovial and polite, he became very popular with early morning customers, one of whom – the Chief Constable – warned him about the impending conflict. 'Rudolf, you'd better get off back to Germany, it looks like war,' he urged.

'I not go,' responded Henniger.

'Come Rudolf,' prompted the Chief half in jest, 'don't you want to fight for the Kaiser?'

The answer could not have been plainer: 'Bugger de Kaiser!'

Unfortunately, such vehemency could not save poor Rudolf from the mob. Knowing he was a German, they smashed his windows and looted his stock, only refraining from torching the shop and imperilling Frau Henniger - his English born wife - and her two cowering babies for fear of setting the whole street ablaze. Rudolph was interned in the Isle of Man by the friendly Chief Constable, his wife fleeing by night to her native city of Birmingham, where she obtained work at the BSA factory in Small Heath. Within a day of her starting her new employment, however, the entire workforce downed tools, vowing they would not tolerate 'bloody Huns'. Mrs Henniger's seriously wounded brother left his military hospital to try to reason with the strikers but

A Quick Change of Front. (LMA)

they threatened to lynch him, the terror and the stoppage attracting only mild criticism from the press.

A WHALE OILED MACHINE

Under the Munitions of War Act, Smith's Stamping Works became an integral part of the war machine, the company coming under official government control on 6 March 1915. Realizing inefficiencies that necessitated sending drop forgings to Sheffield for further treatment, the company improved its capabilities at the Red Lane plant. Three chamber furnaces and one gas chamber were installed to manufacture cutter brackets for minesweeper paravanes and components for aircraft, together with a large quenching tank containing viscous and pungent whale oil. Operatives referred to this as 'The Fish Shop'. Before the end of 1917, a 7½-acre factory extension in Ribble Road, Gosford Green, was built, housing six batteries of 3-ton hammers that pounded away, booming all day and all night.

HE CYCLED TO WORK WITH ALL HIS TOOLS

'It was Jack Matthews who got me to go as an apprentice bricklayer in 1911 at Tom Hancock's & Co in Coventry where I worked until I joined the Royal Engineers in 1915. I had 3 shillings a week and I had to find my bicycle, my brick hammer, trowel and all my tools. I cycled to Coventry every day.'

(Recollections of Ernest Gazey of Colliers Oak Farm, Fillongley, eight miles from Coventry. From *I Remember Strawberries & Sewage*, compiled from oral recordings by Susan K More.)

PREMATURE RETIREMENT FOR CITY NAGS

Shortly after the declaration of war, the city's oldest family printing and box-making company, Bushills, modernised and bought a motor van. The vehicle was immediately commandeered for the war effort so the firm had to revert to age-old transport. Their ancient cart pulled by two stout horses was once again brought into service, regularly making the thirty-six miles round trip between Coventry and Birmingham in one day.

(During the war, Bushills made cartons for munitions but mainly produced vast quantities of food packaging to supply the army with wrapped convenience food.)

MISSING THE BUSES

On 30 March, Coventry's first motorbus service was inaugurated, connecting Stoke Heath with central East Street and Hales Street, using six new open-topped, thirty-four seat double decker vehicles manufactured by Maudslay. Before a shot had been fired, the bus frames were impressed under war powers and the bodies were sold to Sheffield Corporation. 'When's the next tram?'

EMPTY SHELVES

'The rush to the shops has been enormous. People who should have known better began to buy up provisions to last them, in some cases, for many months. People should not replenish the larders of one class at the expense of poor citizens. Every household should guard against selfish hoarding.'

(Coventry Mayor Siegfried Bettmann speaking on 7 August. A German by birth, Bettmann was a naturalised Briton and founder of the *Triumph Company*. Public opinion about his ethnicity eventually forced him from office.)

Bettmann was the first non-British born man to hold the position of Mayor and one of only a few ethnic Germans to avoid internment. He married a local woman, Anne Meyrick, joined the Liberal Party and become a local councillor and a JP.

Two weeks after the declaration of war, he received an urgent telephone call from the Army Service Corps asking his company to provide one hundred Triumph motorcycles for the British Expeditionary Force for delivery to an army camp in the south of England within twenty-four hours. Despite it being a Saturday, he mobilized his workers and the order was despatched from Coventry Railway Station for delivery on time. But this obvious commitment to his adopted home did not help counter the prejudice and hysteria directed at all things German. Bettmann lost his chairmanships of the Triumph and Gloria and the Standard Motor companies, he had to resign from the Cycle Manufacturers Union - an organisation he had founded - and there was a scurrilous and libellous vendetta waged against him, fomented by articles in the *Daily Mail*. Bettmann sued the newspaper in the courts, who upheld his action and awarded him damages of 140 guineas.

Undaunted, Bettmann continued to support the war effort, arranging for the unoccupied Whitley Abbey to be put to use as accommodation for Belgian refugees. He subscribed £250 to the Prince of Wales' National Relief Fund and his wife involved herself in a similar initiative on behalf of the British Red Cross Society appeal. In that personally tormented year of 1914, Bettmann established the Annie Bettmann Foundation, primarily to assist ex-servicemen with business start-up finance. The organisation still exists today and has been expanded to help students.

Bettmann truly earned his Coventrian status, dying at his Elm Bank, Stoke Park, home in 1951.

WE'RE ONLY HERE FOR THE BEER

Coventry consumers worried about the dwindling stocks of food, but they were also concerned that the beer pumps would run dry. A 1914 postcard shows a hundred strong queue of thirsty people snaking from the door of the Clarence Inn Stores – an 'outdoor only' establishment – in Earlsdon Avenue. Its publican was the famous trick cyclist Sam Brown. He performed stunts on the amazing 'Eiffel Tower Cycle', specially built by the Humber Cycle Company and resembling 'one side of a coal pit head gear'.

THE FIRES ARE LIT

'You can't remember 1914. I can. When the murder at Sarajevo happened no one had any idea the fires were lit all over the world.'

(Comments of famous Warwickshire authoress and suffragist Mary Dormer Harris. In anticipation of air raids, Harris was charged in 1916 with the removal of the Coventry archives to a place of safety in the local vaults of Lloyds Bank.)

HOSPITAL PREPARES

At the outbreak of war, the Coventry and Warwickshire Hospital allocated thirty beds in anticipation of military casualties. The provision soon proved to be inadequate and appeals were made for funds to allow immediate expansion. Industrialist Alfred Herbert responded to the call and immediately despatched a telegram: 'Hearing that it is desired to provide for a large number of wounded soldiers, I offer, on behalf of my company, a contribution of £1000 towards the expenditure.' The generous gift was accepted and the expansion took place, a new ward bearing the name of the benefactor.

(The hospital dealt with a total of 2,500 cases during the war.)

CRISIS IN THE SHOPS

'The legend 'Business as Usual' was displayed in many shop windows, only to be laughed at and it proved to be futile in allaying pessimistic apprehensions. Such a war had not been thought possible and, at its starting, there was general consternation. Prices began to rise, stocks were withheld in hopes of greater gain, visitors to the seaside hurriedly returned and the idea spread that British people were threatened with starvation. For a time there was something in the nature of panic; shops were besieged by customers and inordinate quantities of goods sought to be purchased for filling the larders. Usually cool-headed Co-operative housewives became alarmed and the crisis was worsened by multiple buying. Sugar supplies became most difficult. Then coal became a 'burning' subject, for little could be obtained to burn. There were accumulations at collieries but railway rolling stock could not be liberated by the authorities to convey it to the places where it was wanted.' (Coventry Perseverance Co-operative Society.)

A COVENTRY HEROINE

Selina Dix, the Headmistress of the progressive Wheatley Street School, became an influential member of the local Food Control Committee as well as a leader of the committee supervising the administration of the newly enacted Education (Provision of Meals) Act of 1914. With a passion for domestic science and good nutrition, she became an educational pioneer who regularly provided wholesome breakfasts for her pupils long before the free schools meals service came into being. With drive and personal initiative, she set up a communal kitchen in Ford Street, supervising the preparation of meals for distribution to four additional centres. She supervised care for young refugees from Belgium at her school and organized collections of money to fund foreign schemes to alleviate the distress of child victims of the war. A true patriot and Coventry heroine, she was awarded an MBE in 1918 and her work was also recognised by the Russian government, who presented her with a citation and a medal.

LOOP LINE EASES CONGESTION

On 16 August, the Coventry Loop Line was opened to ease congestion through Coventry Station, taking goods traffic onto the Rugby main line. The new line served two goods yards, the Wholesale Market and the Coventry Ordnance Works.

THE RAPE OF LOUVAIN

In a five-day orgy of destruction, looting and murder, hundreds of men, women and children were butchered by German forces in the Belgian town of Louvain, commencing on 25 August. Around 2,000 buildings were destroyed, 300,000 ancient manuscripts and mediaeval books were burnt, the university and church of St Pierre were badly damaged by fire and 10,000 people, more or less the entire population, were expelled. The atrocities were condemned across the world, editors struggling to find words to describe the depravity and the barbaric and hideous treatment of civilians. One quoted motorcycle despatch rider said: 'In the market place of Gembloux, I saw the body of a woman pinned to the door of a house by a sword driven through the chest. The body was naked and the breasts had been cut off.'

'RUFUS' AVOIDS CONSCRIPTION

'I am told that my pony carthorse 'Rufus' is not likely to be commandeered yet as chestnut horses are not taken at first, their colour being too conspicuous.'

(21 August diary entry by Cordelia Leigh of Stoneleigh Abbey. The army acquired 469,000 equines within the United Kingdom in the period 1914-20 and many more from other countries. By 1917, there were over one million horses and mules in service. During the years of attrition, 484,000 animals succumbed; 210 were killed by poison gas. One horse or mule was lost for every two men.)

PEEPING TOM?

Army veterinary personnel began scouring the countryside around Coventry seeking suitable equine conscripts for the cavalry. In September, word reached John Townshend in the Coleshill area that the inspectors' arrival was imminent. So he took action. With two helpers, he blindfolded his favourite horse, Tom, and managed to smuggle him up the external staircase of a granary opposite Gilson Hall. The bemused Tom was led into an upper room deeply scattered with straw and told to keep quiet. The vets arrived, inspected other horses assembled below and took several away. But there was not a peep from Tom and he was saved. (Retold from a story by Joy Wright in *The Townshend Chronicles*.)

NEW STREETS SCHEME SHELVED

In October, the outbreak of hostilities forced the city council to postpone its ambitious plans for the redevelopment of the city centre. Costing an estimated £300,000 (currently £28 million), the scheme was designed to ease congestion and modernize the mediaeval street plan, one councillor commenting: 'Into a city that was built for 20-30,000 people they were crushing about 120,000'.

WAR IS MOST UNHOLY

'Whatever you might think of the cause of the war, I tell you that the working men of this country, France and Germany are being used as tools of a ring of financiers. There is an organized campaign going on just now of putting the German workman in the light of the wild beast, assassinating women and children. I refuse to believe that the men of the German Social Democratic Party, whom I would be proud to shake by the hand, had suddenly become assassins and monsters as is painted by the press. We are not in the war because it is righteous – no war was ever a righteous one – and not because it is holy, for war is most unholy. There is one single power which can prevent a further repetition of this and that is the power of democracy.'

(Extract from a 27 October campaign speech by Mr R.C. Wallhead, prospective Labour candidate for Coventry.)

WOMEN WEAR THE TROUSERS

During the long winter, Ada Bonham and her sister, Mrs Carpenter, were recruited to crew the open-topped tramcars that operated in the city, taking turns at driving and conducting. Wearing long, ankle length skirts, they were hampered in collecting fares in wet weather, having to ascend metal stairs to the top-deck, where passengers sheltered under umbrellas. So they complained. The operating company responded by obtaining two pairs of rather ugly heavy twill trousers from a cavalry regiment.

RECRUITMENT EPIDEMIC

On 3 December, thousands of excited Daimler workers marched from their factory to the recruiting office in Coventry city centre, the mass of cheering and exultant men filling the thoroughfare from the top of Bishop Street to the end of Broadgate. An improvised band led the cavalcade, a young wag striding out in front banging a kettle drum, other men blowing bugles and tin whistles and some rattling empty tin cans.

The recruitment momentum was sustained until October 1915, when Lord Derby introduced a new initiative directed at encouraging even more men to enlist.

> 'No such scenes were ever before witnessed in English history', noted an incredulous reporter. 'The rush of men to be attested under Lord Derby's scheme seems to have been epidemic. Men were signed up in batches of one hundred, while in the workshops themselves equally large numbers were attested.'

Recruits were encouraged by the 2s 9d signing up fee but some were not so enthusiastic and ugly scenes ensued. Belligerent factory workers threatened to down tools if their colleagues refused the call to arms. Others trundled reluctant co-workers through the factory in wheelbarrows with malevolent threats and accusations of cowardice.

THE GERMANS RUN AWAY SQUEALING

> 'On December 7, we paid a visit to Mr Phillips' Private Hospital for wounded soldiers at Coventry. Mr & Mrs Phillips have given up part of their house and take ten wounded privates and a nurse. The soldier we saw had his finger shot off at Ypres. He did not speak as if the German private soldiers were specially brave as a whole; he said they can only be induced to charge if they were drunk and will not advance except in closed up companies; if any get separated from their company and are fired upon, they run away 'squealing'. They get easily excited, whereas our men keep their heads.' (Diary of Cordelia Leigh.)

BUSINESS AS USUAL
DURING ALTERATIONS
TO THE MAP OF EUROPE

Sign in a local tailor's shop.

Batt's had everything for the soldier at Christmas. (LMA)

FROM BIKES TO BULLETS

From his factory in Spon Street, innovative engineer and industrialist James Buckingham produced fifteen vehicles per week during the year, including light cars and his famous 'CHOTA CYCLECAR – THE FASTEST CYCLE ON THE ROAD'. Later, he went on to invent and produce an incendiary bullet specifically designed to shoot down zeppelins and observation balloons, supplying twenty-six million bullets by the end of the conflict. His contribution to the war effort was eventually recognised by the award of an OBE.

DAIMLER DELIVERS

By the end of the year, the Daimler factory had produced 100 BE2c aircraft. Test flights were conducted from its strip, which would eventually become Radford Aerodrome in 1917. Some dare devil pilots flew dangerously low over the munitions works, hoping to impress the girls on their tea breaks, one local resident noting: 'Yesterday another aeroplane came down bang and the lieutenant was killed. That makes six more fellows who have been burnt to death around here in the last three weeks.'

The factory also manufactured engines for field artillery tractors and built engines for the 'Little Willie' and 'Big Willie' tanks.

COVENTRY'S MOST COLOURFUL CHARACTER
In 1914, attracted by burgeoning job prospects, Yorkshireman Albert Smith arrived in Coventry from Keighley and began working as a crane driver for Alfred Herbert. This extrovert boxer, athlete, showman, charlatan and show-off immediately imposed himself on the local scene and became a well known character in the local pubs. He sold cough lozenges in the city bars, feigning voice loss, until one of his miracle tablets restored his speech and he also preached in the Market Square, unsuccessfully standing on one occasion as a local MP. Smith's most celebrated escapade, however, was to dive from the parapet of the Brandon Viaduct, completing two double somersaults before splashdown in the River Avon.

BREAD AND LICE
'The total number of children who were fed during 1914 was 983; the number receiving meals at any one time varied from 5 to 439. There were 3241 meals provided. The meals are provided at four schools, forming centres for groups of schools. The breakfasts consist of half a pint of cocoa and one 6oz roll (plain roll with butter or jam or currant roll on alternate days) per child. On Wednesdays, porridge with roll is substituted for the above. The cost of breakfast is 1½d per meal. Owing to the outbreak of war and the consequent increase in the number of children requiring meals, an Investigative Officer was appointed to enquire into the circumstances of every family whose children were receiving free meals.

'There were 568 cases of head and body lice reported. The cleansing department continues to meet an unfortunate great need in Coventry. In spite of teaching and all the cleansing work that has been done, no diminution of the numbers of verminous children can be perceived.' (Annual Health Report.)

KEEP YOUR CHINS UP!

In almost every edition during 1914, the *Coventry Graphic* sought to raise a laugh, publishing a series of lampooning quips and cartoons such as:

'The Kaiser has dispensed with the enormous spike in his helmet. He will now be able to talk through his hat better.'

Trench cartoon of the Kaiser.
(Courtesy Pat Warren)

'A Berlin paper refers to the Kaiser's Throne Room. It will soon be the Thrown-Out Room.'

'I understand there is no truth in the rumour that Admiral Von Tirpitz has threatened to bale out the Atlantic with a bucket thus making it a walk-over.'

'Will correspondents please note that further references to the Kurds having been driven a whey is prohibited.'

OWED (ODE?) TO THE CENSOR

'The Army has suffered a rout,
In a battle at … (name scrubbed out).
The enemy soon were defeated,
By the work of the … (regiment deleted).
They had just turned the enemy flank,
Near the banks of the river … (left blank).
And the Allies then without rest,
Commenced shelling at … (target suppressed).
If the censor any more names erases,
Quite frankly <u>he shall</u> go to blazes!'

I'M OK

'I bought four silk postcards to send home and I sent one straightaway, but it was censored and destroyed. They were worried that the ship would be torpedoed and they'd give information away to the Germans. The other three I just wrote on them 'OK Ralph.' (Private Ralph Miller –1/8th Battalion Royal Warwickshire Regiment.)

French embroidered 'KEEP ME IN YOUR HEART' greeting card sent from the front on 27 July 1918 and signed 'Daddy'.(LMA)

RADICAL JACK

Following his resounding victory at the Battle of Coronel off the southern coast of Chile, an emboldened Admiral Graf Maximilian von Spee sailed south, targeting merchant and troop shipping in the South Atlantic. He steamed towards Port Stanley in the Falkland Islands, intending to attack the British radio and coaling station. Unbeknown to the German High Command, the First Sea Lord, Admiral Jack Fisher, had despatched a flotilla of warships to intercept the raiders, the ultra modern and fast battle cruisers *Invincible* and *Inflexible* leading a squadron of ships that engaged the enemy to devastating effect. Out manoeuvred and outgunned on 8 December, the Germans lost four cruisers – the *Scharnhorst*, the *Gneisenau*, the *Nurnberg* and the *Leipzig* and 2,200 men. Ten British seamen died. The victory boosted morale across the nation, the people of Coventry remembering a former pupil of King Henry VIII's School – 'Radical Jack' - who was regarded by some as the greatest admiral since Nelson.

(Following the atrocity off the Old Head of Kinsale the following year, Admiral Fisher said this: 'This *Lusitania* business is shocking. Unofficially, we are telling you … take no prisoners from U-boats. Thou shalt not kill but needst not strive officiously to keep alive. Moderation in war is imbecility. Hit first, hit hard, hit anywhere.')

A VERY MERRY CHRISTMAS

'We set off for the trenches at 6.30 pm, a little sad at spending Christmas Day in them. They said: 'You come halfway and we will come halfway and bring some cigars.' This went on for some time. They had a stove with a teapot singing away and altogether it was a most enjoyable evening – a very merry Christmas and a most extraordinary one…but I doubled the sentries after midnight.' (Diary of Captain Robert Hamilton of the 1st Battalion Royal Warwickshire Regiment, in the trenches near St Yvon – entry for 24 December.)

CHAPTER 2

1915:
Keep the Home Fires Burning

They were summoned from the hillside,
They were called in from the glen,
And the country found them ready,
At the stirring call for men.

Let no tears add to the hardship,
As the soldiers pass along,
And although your heart is breaking,
Make it sing this cherry song:

Keep the home fires burning,
While your hearts are yearning,
Though the lads are far away,
They dream of home.

There's a silver lining,
Through the dark clouds shining,
Turn the dark clouds inside out,
Till the boys come home.

THE DARKEST CITY IN ENGLAND
Following the first Zeppelin raid on King's Lynn and Yarmouth in January, which killed ten people, orders were given to dig shelters,

install warning sirens and impose blackout restrictions, Coventry quickly earning the reputation as the darkest city in England. Anti-aircraft batteries and searchlights were set up outside the Shepherd and Shepherdess pub in Keresley and they were also deployed in Wyken, Hearsall Common and Whitley Water Works. The task of intercepting the raiders was given to two fighter aircraft based at a temporary field in Rugby. Unfortunately, the two pilots insisted on enjoying the comforts of their officers' mess in Castle Bromwich and had to be scrambled from their beds some thirty miles distance. Drake finishing his game of bowls it was not!

A WAY WITH THE GIRLS

'Girls, as with men, like to be treated courteously, and, of course, are entitled to be. To joke and jest with them is a mistake; discipline suffers. Discipline is not easy to maintain. But like all things, a proper beginning is a must. I always wish my girls a good morning when they come into the shop but I never hold conversations with them except upon their work. I am always ready to listen to what they have to say and I am always civil. These are my methods and I find them successful.' (Munitions factory foreman.)

KHAKI COVENTRY

Contingents of the Royal Munster Fusiliers and the South Wales Borderers arrived in chilly Coventry on 11 January, some still in tropical uniforms and sporting unseasonal tans. Part of a vast assembly of men returning from active service across the empire, these troops were found temporary accommodation across the city. Although there was an element of coercion and compulsion about billeting, most residents did their bit, receiving a welcome board and lodging allowance of 17 shillings and 6 pence per week for each soldier. Officers were housed for 3 shillings per night but were expected to pay an additional sum for food. Many of the soldiers, who were described as 'big, rough fellows who were always ready for a scrap', were billeted in Earlsdon, Chapelfields and Pool Meadow, local publicans being warned about the prevalence of drunkenness after six men were arrested for being 'frightfully drunk' on the first night! Within a few days, however, the generally good humoured, helpful and honest soldiers were warmly accepted into the community, some local girls embarking on whirlwind romances leading to lifetime friendships and marriage.

In a largely secret ceremony on 12 March, King George V inspected elements of the soon-to-be-legendary 1st Battalion Royal Munster Fusiliers, 29th Division, at the Fosse Way/London Road crossroads near the village of Stretton-on-Dunsmore. The *Coventry Herald* published a photograph of the event but gave no locational details to accord with censorship regulations. Some days later, the troops left Coventry for undisclosed destinations. Led by a marching band and accompanied by Buller – a bull terrier presented to the battalion by the residents of Earlsdon - the battalions strode through the thronged streets to wild cheering and applause, local people, tumultuous but often tearful, thrusting flowers, chocolates, oranges and cigarettes into grateful hands. The men departed in three trains, leaving Coventry in somewhat stunned silence.

Taken before the regiment left Coventry, a posed photograph of somewhat glum and disinterested Royal Munster Fusiliers' officers and local officials standing with the landlord of the Royal Oak – W Mayor. But Buller looks up for it. The mascot was caparisoned in a khaki coat for weekdays and a braided emerald green coat for Sundays. Both coats were embroidered with the Coventry coat of arms on one side and the Munsters' regimental badge on the other. Buller was allocated a billet allowance of 8 shillings and 9 pence per week. (Courtesy Herbert Art Gallery & Museum).

On 25 April, the Royal Munster Fusiliers stormed V Beach on the Gallipoli Peninsula in one of the most inept and ultimately futile attacks in the history of the war. Buller leapt onto the beach in a hail of bullets and survived unharmed, the campaign claiming a shivering 34,011 British troops killed (a total of at least 114,00 men were lost) by the time the 29th Division was withdrawn in January 1916. The architect of the debacle? Winston Churchill.

BELGIAN REFUGEES FIND A HOME
The whole of the Whitley Abbey estate was transferred to the Coventry Refugee Committee for the use of Belgian refugees, numbers ranging from seventy to a hundred individuals and families. The estate was supervised by a contingent of sisters from the Ursulines of Puers convent in Antwerp led my Mère Marguerite. The chapel attached to the premises was overseen by Abbé van Heyst, who ably guided the spiritual life of hundreds of his fellow Belgians who were scattered around the city.

BELGIAN CHIDREN EXCEL IN SCHOOL
Eighty Belgian children in three classes were educated in Wheatley Street School under the direction of headmistress Dix. After just nine months, most were proficient in the new language and were able to

This plaque in St Mary's Guildhall was presented to the city of Coventry in 1918. (LMA)

Cigarette cards were produced by the million during the war and many were collected by soldiers and their families. Such was the variety of subjects covered that the cards became known collectively as 'The Working Man's Encyclopaedia'. The cards shown here were issued in 1915 by WD & HO Wills, the fifty scenes in the series depicting Gems of Belgian Architecture. As the Tommy's lit their fags, they must have wondered if all the featured buildings would suffer the fate of the Ypres Cloth Hall and Belfry (No 4 in the series bottom right), which was totally destroyed by artillery fire. (LMA)

pass for English pupils, one boy standing up in form and singing rousing choruses of *God Save the King* and *Tipperary*. The children were also taught French and Flemish. It was noted that they were perplexed and upset at the employment of corporal punishment, as it was unknown in the Belgian educational system.

TOBACCO FOR THE WARWICKS

'Thanks to the generosity of our readers, the Warwickshire RHA in France will receive in the next few days a parcel containing

1600 ozs of good tobacco and 200 briar pipes.' (*The Coventry Graphic* 22 January.)

COVENTRY LADIES ROLL THEIR SLEEVES UP

In January, a Voluntary Aid Detachment hospital was opened at Hillcrest in Radford Road, local ladies giving their free time to care for sick and injured soldiers. Created before the war, VADs supplemented the major medical centres and were set up in church and village halls and large private homes such as the historic Guy's Cliffe near Warwick, its music, drawing and dining rooms becoming medical wards. Ladies cooked, washed, scrubbed and cleaned, lit fires and undertook basic nursing duties such as applying bandages and changing dressings. The first Coventry patients were men from the Munsters and South Wales Borderers.

By 1916, Hillcrest had served 627 patients, offering fifty five beds in eight wards, one of them in the open air. The hospital was generously supported by donations from the Coventry public. It had a gymnasium in its grounds, an attractive garden, with facilities for quoits and croquet and a popular billiard room. Some patients grew vegetables and reared chickens, others made baskets and carpets.

ILLUMINATING COMPLAINT

'Now that the reduction in street lighting is in force, to go from the city centre outwards is to face an uninviting prospect … it was impossible to see a person two yards away. If there is a danger in lighting the streets it might be thought that the brilliant lights proceeding from elevated factories would also constitute a danger. At present, they can be seen from a great distance and, indicating as they do the importance of industrial centres, they mark the position of the city more surely than street lights ever can.' (The *Coventry Graphic* 7 February.)

'Landed on Turkish soil under a terrific fire from enemy entrenchments. Battalion lost about seventeen killed and 200 wounded. I lay in the open from 7 am to 5 pm and did not get a scratch. Dug ourselves in that night snipers going all night but we did not return their fire. Food for twenty-four hours – two biscuits and some water. '

(Extract from the diary of Corporal Denis Moriarty, of the 1st Battalion Royal Munster Fusiliers.)

LAST LETTER HOME
Some of the bitterest fighting of the war took place on the battlefield at Ypres in April. The 1st Battalion Royal Welsh Fusiliers met desperate German resistance and was forced to retreat, the Commanding Officer's last screamed order, 'everyman for himself', propelling the remnants of a force of 300 men back to the trenches. Twenty-two year old Albert Troughton managed to escape but news of the deaths of comrades and the hideous experience of combat left him in a daze. Shell shocked, he wandered off. He was later arrested, returned to his unit and charged with desertion. No witnesses could help in his defence. They were either dead or captured as prisoners. Albert was summarily court-martialed but did not take advantage of a prisoner's friend. His exemplary previous army service was not taken into account and he was sentenced to be shot at dawn, the commanding general confirming the death sentence 'as a deterrent to others'.

On the night of 21 April 1915, Private Albert Troughton scribbled his last letter home to his family in Coventry his army gaolers risking charges by agreeing to send the message on. The condemned man's last words were: 'I am dying tomorrow, please clear my name'.

The letter reads:

Dear Mother and Father, Sisters and Brothers,

Just a few lines to let your know I am in the best of health and hope you are mother. I am sorry to have to tell you that I am to be shot tomorrow at 7 o'clock in the morning the 22nd April. I hope you will take it in good part and not upset yourself. I shall die like a soldier, so goodbye mother, father, sisters and brothers, if any left. Remember me to Mr Kendell and them who knew me. Mother I am very sorry nothing happened to me at Ypres, I should not have went away and then I might have stood a good chance of being still alive, but I think that they are paying the debt at the full rate. I thought the most they would give me would be about ten years. It is worse than waiting to be hung.

I hope you got my letters; which I sent you while waiting for my court martial. It seems that something told me I would be shot, so I think the time has come for me to die… I am only a common soldier and all civilians should know that I have fought for my country in hail, sleet and snow. To the trenches we have to go. All my comrades have been slaughtered which I think everyone should know. When our regiment was captured, the Colonel loudly strained "Everyone for himself", but on and on I fought and got clear of the German trenches. This is the punishment I get for getting clear of the Germans…. I have wrote my last letter to you all at home, so mother don't be angry with me because I have gone to rest, and pray for me, and I will pray for you. Remember me to Mr Newbold and tell him about it… I have been silly to go away but if you knew how worried I was, and almost off my head. Think how we had been slaughtered at the beginning of the war… You think they would have a bit of pity for those who are living for their country. Goodbye to all at home. Goodbye, Goodbye.

From your Son, Albert.

(Albert was one of 306 men executed by firing squad during the war. The Shot at Dawn Campaign still works tirelessly to obtain well-overdue pardons. The men are remembered in the National Memorial Arboretum in Alrewas Staffordshire, a sculpture of 17 year old Private Herbert Burden - who had lied about his age to enlist - fronting 306 wooden posts. Albert is buried in Estaires Communal Cemetery, Belgium.)

LOST ON THE *LUSITANIA*

On 7 May at 2.10 pm, Kapitan-Leutnant Walther Schweiger of the German submarine U-20 fired a single torpedo at the cruise liner

Lusitania. Nearly at the end of her journey from New York, the ship sank in less than twenty minutes, eleven miles from the Old Head of Kinsale off the southern Irish port of Queenstown. From a total complement of 1959 passengers and crew, 1198 people died. One of them was Walter Wright, from Stoke Park in Coventry, who occupied first class cabin B-102 (ticker number 46166), attended by steward Percy Penny. A manager with the Dunlop Rim and Wheel Company, Wright sailed to the United States on business in January, cabling his wife with details of his homecoming. He never returned and his body was never found. Coventry relatives, friends and colleagues erected a memorial to Walter in the London Road Cemetery.

Two months later, on 3 August, when seething anger at the sinking had subsided to one of smouldering bitterness, *The Times* newspaper published the text of a popular song by Rudolf Kühn that was doing the rounds of German variety theatres:

THE DESTRUCTION OF THE *LUSITANIA*

Carrying shameful contraband,
From New York to the English land,
Bearing thousands on she came,
But the U-boat sniffed its game.

Sailed the *Lusitania* gay,
Farther on her felon way,
Off Ireland's coast the U-boat peers,
See the course her quarry steers!

Passengers from every shore,
English, Greek and Dutch galore,
Americans and sons of France,
Sail along to death's fell dance.

Ah! the U-boat's aim was good,
Who doesn't choke drowns in the flood.
Vanderbilt was there that day,
The only one we missed was Grey.

Each one gives his nose a wrench,
All the gases awful stench.

'They're our shells, our very own',
Cries the Yankee Mr Kohn.

The old water nymphs below,
Straight begin to curse and blow.
What chuck ye down so carelessly,
On the bottom of the sea?
There lay the dead in Neptune's jaws,
Most of them with scalded paws,
Sons of England with their wives,
Ne'er so still in all their lives!

Chant we now the funeral chant,
More U-boats is what we want,
To a chill grave with the enemy,
Till he stop bothering Germany.

WOVEN IN SILK
R.M.S. LUSITANIA.

| Length 790 ft. | Breadth 88 ft. | Depth 60 ft. | Displacement 45,000 tons. |

This beautifully embroidered 'stevengraph' card was produced by Coventry firm Thomas Stevens. (Courtesy Herbert Art Gallery & Museum).

On reading the vile words, thousands of readers went blue with rage and choked on their porridge (if they could get it).

Further outrage at the atrocity helped bring the United States into the war, some commentators suggesting that the attack was deliberately encouraged by Churchill to bring about that end.

KNITTING IS FITTING
In the Barr's Hill School for Girls magazine for May, alongside a list of hockey fixtures, several published poems with evocative titles such as *The Fairy Queen's Wedding* and announcements naming the prizewinners in the Pressed Flower Competition, was the following discreet entry:

'Comforts For The Troops
Upper V – 10 pairs of mittens, 10 helmets, 10 scarves, 3 pairs of socks and 1 pair of cuffs.
Lower IV – 10 pairs of mittens, 14 pairs of socks, 6 scarves, 8 helmets and 1 pair of bed socks.
Lower III's – 6 pairs of mittens, 5 scarves, 1 pair of cuffs and 3 body belts.'

(Barr's Hill School – the first private school for girls in Coventry – was opened in 1908. In contrast to the martial tones of similar publications recording the activities of pupils at boys' schools (most had active Cadet Corps), the contents of its magazine are indicative of a protective and sheltering regime.)

LOOK … AN AIRSHIP!
'I was in Ashow School this morning when an airship went over and all the children rushed out to see it except one little girl who remained in her seat and cried, to the great amusement of the others.' (1 June entry in the diary of Cordelia Leigh of Stoneleigh Abbey.)

THE KING COMES TO TOWN
On 22 July, amidst a not-so-dark news blackout, the King visited Coventry, alighting in the rain to the cheers of 500 people. He was met by the sombre mayor and other councillors at the railway station, his

*King George V inspecting munitions. (*www.gwpda.org/photos)

motorcade proceeding first to the Coventry Ordnance Works, where he met representatives of the 6121 men and 1341 women employees, seeing examples of their work including naval guns, howitzers, field artillery, aircraft, cartridges and shells. Later, he inspected the production lines at Daimler, Herbert and Rover.

BOOMING COVENTRY

'Outside the naval shop near Swan Lane was an immense cast-iron firing pit for testing the guns before despatch. When this was in operation, it could be heard all over Stoke and Foleshill and further. The huge guns were capable of shooting a 16-inch shell 22 miles.' (Marguerite Thorn.)

WAR GAMES

'Thursday – This day was set apart by the powers that be (i.e. the Colonel and officers) for the annual field day. The park is admirably suited to military manoeuvres and an exciting, realistic effect was produced. The usual mock battle took place – shots ringing out on all sides; the enemy moving in the bracken with only their heads showing or quickly rushing across the open stretches; officers and NCOs giving orders to their respective units – in fact, the atmosphere of battle, stern and grim – but without the pathetic sight of cries of wounded and dying – permeated the whole proceedings.'

(Report of proceedings at the Bablake School Annual Cadet Camp at Stoneleigh in August.)

A naval gun on it way to the shipyard. (Courtesy Herbert Art Gallery & Museum).

TURN OFF THE LIGHT!

On 19 September, a passing night duty policeman entered the premises of Arthur Stanton of 55 Stoney Stanton Road, Coventry and cautioned the occupant for failing to screen a bedroom window. The miscreant was later summoned to a hearing by magistrates and pleaded guilty to the charge, explaining that he failed to turn off the light to allow his wife to bring gruel to his sickbed. He was fined £1.

FIRE! FIRE!

Coventry Fire Brigade were summoned to a fire at the Exhall Colliery near Nuneaton on 21 September. The blaze was caused by the accidental knocking over of a lit paraffin lamp, the flame quickly igniting pitch pine shaft fittings. Asphyxiating smoke spread rapidly throughout the mine and although 375 men managed to escape, fourteen lost their lives.

THAT IN THE OPINION OF THIS HOUSE, THE PRESENT GREAT EUROPEAN WAR WILL NOT BE THE LAST

> 'MR HARRIS, in proposing the motion, said that people could not do without war. History proves from the earliest times that there have always been wars against nations and he saw no reason for their cessation. As there is a quarrelsome member in every family, so there are always nations which adopt aggressive policies, and thus cause wars. He thought that Russia might desire room for expansion in the future and this might lead to friction with Britain. He had no hope whatever that this would prove the last war.'

'MR ALLEN, in opposing, said that the huge losses in men and money, which even the victor must suffer in war, would frighten nations from engaging in them. There would always be groups of allied nations, and this would make easy success impossible. In this future there would be increased commercial intercourse, he considered, and the interests of all countries must become interwoven. Greater luxuries would make people unwilling to engage in all the sacrifices of war, and arbitration courts would probably be established. He thought that the terrible weapons would frighten countries from making war.'

'MR EVANS, said that human nature was the cause of wars, and until divine ideas have been substituted for human ones, they could not cease. Considering all the wars of the past, it would be a miracle if they ended suddenly now. The ambitions of nations must always clash and he thought war was an essential factor to civilisation. He believed that Germany would try to regain her lost colonies by another war. He considered settlements by arbitration impossible and that wars would be necessary to enforce international laws.'

'MR MASON, (President) said he was optimistic as regards the question and that the best way of securing peace was by crushing Germany. Disputes might be settled by arbitration and armaments should be more limited after the war. All reforms, in the end, came suddenly, and therefore a change from a period of countless wars into an age of uninterrupted peace must not be regarded as improbable.'

'DR EILOART, thought that there was too much to be said on either side. He criticized the statement that increased luxuries would prevent wars and thought that a narrow patriotism, fostered by our schools, was one cause of quarrels.'

'On being put to the vote, the motion was carried by fourteen votes to three.'

(Extract from King Henry VIII's School *Coventrian* journal recording a Debating and Literary Society debate held on 9 October.)

NURSE CAVELL SHOT

On 12 October, dedicated nurse and patriot Edith Cavell, the daughter of a vicar from Swardeston in Norfolk, was executed by a German firing squad for treason, the shocking news soon making headlines in Coventry and across the world. The death caused widespread revulsion, gave fuel to the allied propaganda war and helped bring the United States into the conflict. At her court martial, Cavell admitted to helping around 200 Allied soldiers to escape from German occupied Belgium. The British government suggested it could not intervene but the US Legation in Brussels applied diplomatic pressure, contacting the German civil governor Baron Von der Lancken with the following warning:

> 'We remind you of the burning of Louvain and the sinking of the *Lusitania* and tell you that this murder will rank with these two affairs and will stir all civilised countries with horror and disgust.'

The uncompromising governor responded by asserting that he would rather see Miss Cavell shot than have harm come to the humblest German soldier, emphasizing that his only regret was that they had not 'three or four old English women to shoot'.

Before she died, the most prominent female casualty of the war said, 'Patriotism is not enough. I must have no hatred or bitterness towards anyone.'

FROM A HOSPITAL BED

> 'It does seem hard luck that I should be shut up here whilst the lads are out there after our long wait for munitions. I see in the papers that some of the Coventry munitions workers still lose time. Well I know it's hard and they can't understand but if they had been out there for one week, only then would they see day and night that every hour put in means a few more Huns knocked out. But over the last few weeks when the enemy commenced shelling, our lads of the RFA could land over three to their one. We began to thank God that those at home had woken up and the news that is just coming through is the thanks of those lads out there to the workers

at home. I am glad to say that my wound is progressing favourably and I hope soon to be back in Dear Old Coventry.'

(Extract from an October letter from Lance Corporal T.W. Booth in Christchurch Hospital, writing to his parents in Earlsdon.)

COVENTRY VEHICLE CONQUERS THE WORST ROAD IN ENGLAND

Motor manufacturers Singer introduced a new 10-horse power vehicle to their range during 1914. Intended as a troop carrier, it was designed to accommodate eight 11 stone men up the 1 in 9 gradient of Stoneleigh Hill in second gear. The new design was pitted against the worst public road in England in the following March. In atrocious conditions of snow and ice, the vehicle reached the top of the notorious Park Rash, linking Wharfedale and Coverdale in Yorkshire, reaching great speed, which 'bewildered the spectators'. The feat was described in the magazine *Autocar* as 'a remarkable performance'.

Simm's Motor Wheel Scout – the first war vehicle of its type in the world. One of Coventry's less impressive vehicles. (Courtesy Herbert Art Gallery & Museum.)

FOOD PRICES SOAR
By the end of the year, bread had more than doubled in price from 4 pence to 9 pence per 4lb loaf. Farm gate prices for wheat jumped from 35 shillings per quarter to 53 shillings per quarter.

CANINE CONTROL
In a report quantifying the dog population of Coventry, the police recorded a figure of 6473 animals – one dog for every four households. £2,427 7s 6d was collected in licence fees, enabling the city to make a profit on its operation of the dog control scheme. However, notwithstanding the financial success of the operation, it was noted that 578 animals had to be destroyed in the lethal chamber and that what were termed 'home executions' were prevalent, particularly of puppies drowned in the canal and in neighbouring pits, pools and streams. The high cost of a licence and the escalating price of food were both cited as reasons for this.

FESTIVE GALES
During the Christmas period, following the worst gales since March 1896, the outlying roads around Coventry were littered with fallen trees and other debris, severely restricting the passage of vehicles. Early users of the highways, such as milkmen, had to use all their local knowledge to by-pass the obstructions, following field paths and farm tracks.

VERMIN AND HOT AIR
'The trenches were infested with rats and mice, but unfortunately there are even less pleasant vermin to contend with. I understand a small bag of flowers of sulphur hung round the neck is a good precautionary measure. If you come across these or know the best stuff to make them of I should like one. The stuff has to be quite fine, so that the sulphur oozes out very gradually. They can be made double, so that one hangs in front and one behind.'

'The blast of hot air which accompanies the explosion is rather rotten and the row shakes you to pieces. One curious thing I noticed. When one explodes, of course splinters of all shapes

and sizes fly in every direction, each with its own note, so that
the second after, the report sounds like a great brass band.'

(Extracts from October and November letters sent by Second
Lieutenant Roland Mountfort to his mother in Coventry. This former
pupil of the King Henry VIII's School was wounded in the Battle of
the Somme. Seventy seven of his letters survive.)

GUN FODDER

'You there! Don't treat my horses like animals. I can get you
two buggers for a shilling a day ... but horses ... they're eighty
pounds apiece!' (A quartermaster's reprimand overheard
somewhere in France.)

CHAPTER 3

1916:
I Didn't Raise My Boy
to be a Soldier

Ten million soldiers to the war have gone,
Who may never return again.
Ten million mothers' hearts must break,
For the ones who died in vain.
Head bowed down in sorrow in her lonely years,
I heard a mother murmur thru' her tears.

COVENTRY AT SPEED

'An American visitor wishing to be highly complimentary, recently declared that Coventry is more like a new city in the Middle West than any part of England. "The people of Coventry walk quicker than other Englishmen,' he said, 'Everyone seems prosperous. There is a briskness in the very air of the place. Your factories are growing as fast as factories in Detroit – and I cannot say more than that. Everyone is busy and everyone is happy!

'Coventry takes compliments such as this calmly. Its people believe that Coventry has set a pace in the growth of industry that it would be hard even for the West to equal. They point to the new factories springing up in their city today at a speed even Detroit could not exceed. Last summer they cut down the corn to make room for a fresh factory extension. Hundreds of navvies were brought in and housed in big tents on the grounds and the factory was completed in less time it would have taken most manufacturers to discuss the plans. Men say with pardonable exaggeration that the Rudge Whitworth works adds a storey a night to make room for expansion. Everywhere in the city it is the same.

'In one way, Coventry reflects the spirit of the age of speed. One sees more women driving motorcars in the streets than anywhere else. Many of them own their own cars and the well-to-do middle class woman learns to drive her own car as naturally as her sister in the south plays hockey." (*The Times* – 17 January.)

KILL THAT LIGHT!

'The regulations with regard to darkening lights at Coventry and Leamington have been made much stricter lately and we have put shades over some of our passage lights and a kind of brown Holland blind over the top of the large window … as we were told that some of the lights might serve as guides to Zeppelins making for Coventry. Coventry itself is very dark and mysterious looking at night.' (31 January entry in the diary of Cordelia Leigh of Stoneleigh Abbey.)

THE UPSHOT OF DESERTION

In January, Coventry magistrates adjudicated on the case of Private Harry Skelsey of the Royal Warwickshire Regiment. He was charged with attempting suicide by slashing his throat at 37 Sherbourne Street on 1 December 1915. Discharged from hospital on the day prior to his arraignment, Skelsey looked ill and his neck was heavily bandaged. Hearing that the prisoner was an absentee from his regiment, the court remanded Skelsey in custody pending his transfer to the military authorities.

THE FOGS OF WAR

'I have just crossed Great Britain from one end to the other and I have visited innumerable towns and cities. Britain, at last, after more than a year's delay, is mobilized for war. Her achievement today far surpasses the wildest German idea of the 'kolossal'. I have seen factory after factory working steadily 24 hours a day, seven days a week, employing thousands of men and women in making shells, shells, shells! I have seen guns being forged under hydraulic pressure of 12,000 tons; howitzers forged out of the stoutest steel which requires 16 hours in a blast furnace to heat. I have seen motor lorries. They had come across England under their own power and stood ready, waiting to be sent to the front. I have seen dull, brown-coloured, specially constructed staff automobiles lined up ready for shipment; not luxuriously upholstered limousines of peace times but, like part of a true soldier's kit, they are fitted with hard seat cushions of plain leather and steady, small, collapsible tables. I have seen row upon row of motor ambulances of the same brown colour not improvised in construction but especially devised to save the wounded all possible discomfort.

'I have seen shell cases pressed out of the living ingot in less than five minutes and shells forged at a speed three times as great. I have seen smaller shells – chiefly the 18-pounder – turned on the lathe by young girls 16 or 18 years of age, many of them frail, slight girls for whom it was difficult to lift the heavy metal, yet the shells are piled up in pyramids about them on every available space and the pyramids are growing, growing. In one plant, gaily decorated with flags of the Allies, I saw young girls turning out fuses of aluminium and brass. Steadily they worked without looking up from their lathes. Many while working hum a low, crooning tune to mark time with the burrowing note of the knife-edged tool as it cuts deep into the yellow metal.

'I have seen men working at great forges where gun parts are cast, straining every nerve and muscle to accomplish their difficult tasks; handling vast lumps of red-hot metal with lightning dexterity. I have seen machine guns by the hundred and rifles by the thousand, all of most careful workmanship and finish.

'I have seen mile upon mile of khaki cloth being reeled off by looms and thousands of yards of specially prepared white woollen cloth for wrapping propelling charges; hundreds of pairs of knitted khaki puttees patterned by a single cut of the knife. This list might be extended indefinitely.

'The whole North Country has been turned into one vast arsenal. The deep pall of fog and smoke that hangs over the great industrial centres of the Midlands, deeper, denser than it has been for some years past, means that England has at last turned her full energy to the mighty task. The achievement is truly remarkable when it is appreciated that this is only the beginning.' (A correspondent of *The Times* writing in the *Kenilworth Advertiser.*)

A NIGHT AT THE OPERA

'I was on leave from the army when *Il Trovatore* was being performed. Suddenly, the alarm warning of approaching Zeppelins was given and all the lights were switched off. Some disorder appeared imminent among patrons and the leading man, Cynlais Gibbs, appealed for order and threw in a half-hearted witticism. I replied to him in similar vein, and we indulged in several minutes impromptu cross talk. The audience laughed then calmed down while cycle lamps etc were procured to enable the performance to continue. The tenor said he was much obliged to me but the expected 'Zepps' did not appear.'

(Comments of Alderman HBW Cresswell after attending a January performance of Verdi's masterpiece at the Opera House in Hales Street.)

ANGLERS SHIVER

Sponsored by the Earl of Craven, a fishing match took place on 11 March at Coombe Pool, Coombe Abbey, snow and sleet not deterring a sizeable contingent of anglers and spectators. But the fish refused to bite, many fishermen and women keeping dry nets. Two fish totalling 9lb 9oz won the top prize although the special cup provided by the Earl was not awarded. Funds from the sale of tickets and bankside contributions helped swell the coffers of the Soldiers and Sailors Fund.

YOUTHS FINED FOR SLACKING

Twenty one cases were brought before the Coventry Munitions Court on 16 March. In a previously adjourned hearing, a young worker had been given an opportunity to improve his timekeeping but to no avail. In just seven weeks the court was told that the youth had lost a total of fifty four hours. He was reprimanded and fined 30 shillings.

Three boys, whose ages ranged from 15 to 17, pleaded guilty to having played cards in the workshop during working hours. Each boy was fined a week's wages – from £1 to 25 shillings per week – one assessor remarking that the verdict was a lesson in being cruel to be kind.

CONSCRIPTION PANEL KEPT BUSY

The Coventry panel charged with considering the merits of applications seeking exemption from military service were busy again during March. Under cross-examination focusing on his religious beliefs, one conscientious objector was ordered to report for duty, as was a Coventry dentist. The panel had more problems, however, with a third application from a young gipsy. He claimed he was illiterate and had just three weeks schooling in his entire life. He sought exemption on the grounds that he supported his mother. The pair lived in a caravan and earned a nomadic living hawking in the lanes between Berkswell and Birmingham. The panel chairman asked the applicant: 'If I gave you a cheque for £10 what would you do with it?' The gipsy replied: 'I couldn't understand it and should have to leave it to you to do me right'. A temporary certificate was issued, deferring conscription until the end of June.

COVENTRY CHAOS

On Monday 27th March, a driving blizzard brought chaos to Coventry and the surrounding area, blocking rail lines and roads. High winds brought down hundreds of mature trees on the Stoneleigh Estate.

A MIRACULOUS ESCAPE

'I was struck by the bullet on the morning of April 16 and there is little doubt that the tobacco box saved my life. It happened about 7.00 am; we had some trouble with a German sniper ever since daylight and a very good shot he was. He had hit the top of the sandbags about six times and each time he sent a shower of dirt right into our breakfast. Every one of his shots hit about

Example of a smoking box presented to front line soldiers by the Princess Mary's Christmas Fund in 1914. The box's owner was James Cleverley, a cycle fitter from Coventry, who went to France as part of the British Expeditionary Force in September 1914. He was promoted to lance corporal but was wounded in February 1915 and served the rest of the war in England. (Courtesy Herbert Art Gallery & Museum).

the same place. After a time he slackened a little, so, I being the duty sentry at the time, got a periscope to look over the parapet to see if I could locate his position. Just as I was going down to the bottom of the trench, a shot came through the parapet and stuck me over the right breast. It hit the tobacco box, then stuck downwards through my two shirts and just caught my ribs. It was only a scratch. Next morning I found the bullet in my sock where it had fallen overnight.'

(Letter to the *Coventry Graphic* from 28-year-old Ernest Waring of 24 Moat Street, The Butts, Coventry. A photograph of the damaged tobacco box and the German bullet accompanied the published letter. Private Waring was killed shortly after his miraculous escape; and he has no known grave. He is remembered, together with 329 other

Coventry soldiers whose remains were never identified, on the Thiepval Monument on the Somme.)

EASTER UPRISING IN IRELAND

During the Easter holiday, on 24 April, a band of less than 2000 lightly armed Irish patriots seized key locations in Dublin and proclaimed the creation of an Irish Republic independent of the United Kingdom. Within six days, the insurrection was put down and its leaders were executed. Serving in Dublin with the Royal Marine Light Infantry in 190 Brigade Machine Gun Company was Private Harry Jacques from Bell Green Road in Foleshill, Coventry. He was killed in action on the Somme just a few months later, on 13 November.

(Over 20,000 Southern Irish soldiers died fighting for Britain during the First World War but, ironically, Coventry was bombed by the IRA on 25 August 1939, an explosive device planted in a bicycle basket outside the Astley's store in Broadgate killing five civilians and injuring fifty more.)

JUTLAND

Britannia ruled the waves and was determined to maintain her sovereignty of the seas in the first decade of the twentieth century, Britain's strategists and designers, inspired by First Sea Lord, 'Radical Jack' Fisher, embarking on a ship building programme to maintain the status quo and thwart the ambitions of the German navy. In 1907, the world's first battle cruiser – HMS *Invincible* – was launched, becoming, at a single turn of her screws, the fastest capital ship in the world. Dubbed HMS *Uncatchable,* she could glide through the ocean at 28 knots and outrun any comparable ship afloat. But even before she had hit the water, a frenzied arms race had begun, both Britain and Germany spending enormous energy and vast sums of money on fleets of dreadnoughts. German admirals wanted to free the potential blockade of the their ports, wrest control of the Atlantic sea lanes from the British navy and disrupt vital supply lines.   A showdown was inevitable. It came on the morning of 31 May off the north west coast of Denmark, in the vanguard, Rear-Admiral The Honourable Sir Horace Lambert Hood of the illustrious naval family from the ancestral home of Whitley Abbey in Coventry, commanding HMS *Invincible* and bringing his flotilla of ships to action stations. Under the overall command of Admiral Jellico, fifty two British ships opposed forty German vessels commanded by Admiral Scheer.

One hundred and eleven years earlier, the Royal Navy had swept the seas at Trafalgar, the British public expecting every man to do his duty and rout the Germans, although Hipper and the other German commanders had not read the script. In the naval equivalent of hand to hand fighting, the big ships closed to within a few thousands yards, massive guns slicing through metal and lethally detonating turrets and magazines. In a few hours the Royal Navy lost three battle cruisers, three armoured cruisers and eight destroyers, HMS *Invincible* heading the list, which included *Queen Mary*, *Indefatigable*, *Defence*, *Black Prince* and *Warrior*. A total of 6,094 British seamen lost their lives and a further 675 were wounded. The German losses – both in ships and men - were significantly lower.

The end of *Invincible* was particularly catastrophic. Struck by a shell that ignited a magazine, she blew up, the massive explosion breaking her in half. She sank within a few seconds, only six men from a total complement of 1,031 officers and crew surviving. The report of senior surviving officer Commander Hubert Edward Dannreuther makes matter of fact but chilling reading:

SIR,

I DEEPLY regret to report that HMS *Invincible*, commanded by Captain A.L.Cay R.N. and flying the flag of Rear-Admiral the Honourable Horace L. Hood, Rear Admiral Commanding the Third Battle Cruiser Squadron, was blown up and completely destroyed when in action with the enemy at 6.34 p.m. on Wednesday 31 May.

The total number of officers and men on board at the time was 1,031.

The circumstances of the destruction of the ship are briefly as follows:

The *Invincible* was leading the 3rd B.C.S. and at about 5.45 pm first came into action with an enemy light cruiser on the port bow. Several torpedoes were seen coming towards the ship, but were avoided by turning away from them. *Invincible*'s fire was effective on the light cruiser engaged and a heavy explosion was observed. A dense cloud of smoke and steam from this explosion appeared in the same position some minutes later.

Invincible then turned and came into action at about 6.15 pm with the leading enemy battle cruiser, which was thought to be '*Derfflinger*'. Fire was opened at the enemy at about 8,000 yards and several hits were observed.

A few moments before the *Invincible* blew up Admiral Hood hailed the Control Officer in the Control Top from the fore bridge: 'Your firing is very good, keep at it as quickly as you can, every shot is telling'. This was the last order heard from the Admiral or Captain, who were both on the bridge at the end.

The ship had been hit several times by heavy shells but no appreciable damage had been done when at 6.34 pm a heavy shell struck 'Q' turret and, bursting inside, blew the roof off. This was observed from the Control Top. Almost immediately following there was a tremendous explosion amidships indicating that 'Q' magazine had blown up. The ship broke in half and sank in ten or fifteen seconds.

The survivors on coming to the surface saw the bow and stern of the ship only, both of which were vertical and about 50 feet clear of the water.

The survivors were stationed as follows prior to the sinking of the ship:

Commander Dannreuther (Gun Control Officer), C.P.O Thompson, A.B. Dandridge – Fore Control Top.

Yeomanry Signals Pratt – Director Tower Platform.

Lieutenant (T) Sandford – Fore Conning Tower - hatch of which was open.

Gunner Gasson – 'Q' turret at the range finder.

There was very little wreckage, the six survivors were supported by a target life raft and floating timber till picked up by HMS *Badger* shortly after 7 pm.

Only one man besides those rescued was seen to come to the surface after the explosion and he sank before he could reach the target raft.

Commander Hubert Edward Dannreuther.
The news of the multiple sinkings filtered out to a shocked nation, German propaganda inflating the perceived victory to capture headlines

around the world. Questions were asked in Parliament about the British tactics, the poor armour plating of *Invincible* and her sister ships and the role they played in engaging the enemy. Ultimately though, the greatest naval battle of the war persuaded the German navy to resist another all out fleet-to-fleet encounter and to concentrate instead on attrition by submarine, the German navy ignominiously surrendering her capital ships en masse at Scapa Flow at the end of the conflict.

The bodies of Hood and his lost crew were never recovered, grieving friends, relatives and loved ones burying only heartaches in memorial services that took place countrywide. In Coventry, Admiral Hood's demise was modestly celebrated in the affixing of a simple brass plate on the plinth of the family memorial in the London Road Cemetery. The plate commemorating the fourth viscount, who was the nephew of the Honourable AF Gregory-Hood of Stivichall, is fading and weeping now. Perhaps the green and salty tears are for two ships -

Memorial to the Whitley Abbey family of Admiral Hood.(LMA)

Fading plaque honouring Rear Admiral Hood, who in true naval tradition went down with his ship. (LMA)

HMS *Invincible* that sank in 1916 and HMS *Hood*, a vessel that perished in uncannily similar circumstances in 1941?

COVENTRY CAPTURED!

On 22 April, Lieutenant Colonel Charles Coventry of the Egyptian Expeditionary Force was captured by Turkish forces near Katia in Sinai, close to the Suez Canal. This second son of the Earl of Coventry was taken by rail with sixty of his Worcestershire Regiment men to Jerusalem and incarcerated. Detachments of the Warwickshire Yeomanry had also been deployed in the area.

A notable cricketer, Charles Coventry led a colourful life. His death was reported after the South African Jameson Raid of 1896 and a memorial service was arranged at his ancestral home at Earl's Croome Court near Upton on Severn. Just as the eulogies began, news was received that he was alive, prompting a champagne-popping celebration.

For many years, Coventry was the official starter for the Jockey Club. He died at his Worcestershire seat in June 1929.

MOVING PICTURES

A curious diversion in nearby Kenilworth towards the end of May enabled the citizens of Coventry to forget about the war for a while, the London Film Company descending on the ancient castle to shoot a romantic adventure film dubbed *When Knights Were Bold*. Those who could get away from work were entertained with the sight of warriors in full armour, groups of damsels in gorgeous gowns and corpulent monks all acting out a medieval pageant. Twenty eight of the 160 scenes were shot at the castle.

WOULD-BE BANDMASTER JOINS UP AND PLAYS A CALMING TUNE

'My father had made it clear that when I was 19, I was to chose for myself whether I should enlist and serve for the duration of the war. At this time, I was employed in a local solicitor's office.

At the age of 19 I submitted myself for enlistment and passed the medical test in Coventry. But when I arrived at Budbrooke Barracks I was at first rejected by the doctor. After a second examination I was passed for home service. That was in 1916.

'I shall never forget one instance on home service in which my piano playing was useful. We were out signalling from a church tower a few miles from Dover. We could hear an aerial bombardment in progress and we were called back to camp. On the way back my friend and I were called into a house where a young lady was in hysterics owing to the bombardment. We were asked to go in to give her a sense of security. I suppose I saw a piano in the house and I sat down and played *Love's Garden of Roses*, by Haydn Wood. I shall always remember the piece. This seemed to work miracles with the girl. I played a few more songs and she fully quietened down.'

(Recollections of Eric Jordan of Humber Avenue, Coventry. A well-known pianist and entertainer after the war, Eric was secretary of the Coventry Musical Club.)

CONSCRIPTION COMES TO COVENTRY

In May a revised Military Service Act decreed that all men aged between 18 and 41 could be conscripted to the forces. Under the draconian provisions of the act, men who had previously been exempted as unfit were to have their assessments reconsidered. Time expired veterans were also to be called up.

LIMBLESS SOLDIERS VISIT STONELEIGH ABBEY

'Miss Leo Bonn brought over five soldiers, four with only one leg and one with both legs off who moved about on his knees; he was to have artificial legs later. Like all the others he was most cheerful – told us in fits of laughter how, when having a pillow fight with his chums, he forgot that he had no feet - tried to jump on the ground and fell over. 'It was fun,' he said, with a beaming smile.'

*   *   *

```
                    P R O G R A M M E.
                ═*═*═*═*═*═W═*═*═*═*═*

                        Of  The

                "MISS-FIRES" CONCERT PARTY.
                ----------------------------
                Produced  by  Spr.  L.T. Brown, RE.
                          ·*·*·*·*·*·
                        A R T I S T E S:

        L/Cpl. A. Lyn Hardy, A.S.C......Light Comedian.
        Sapper E.W. Budgen,   R.E........Humourist.
        Sergt. A.F.Sutton,    R.E........Comedian.
        Pte. J. Walmsley,     K.O.Y.L.I..Tenor.
        Sapper L.T.Brown,     R.E........Impersonator.
                              ───
                        O R C H E S T R A .
                           ═*═
                    Under the direction of
                Sapper S.V. Eagland (At the Piano).
                               ─
        1st/A.M.F.G.Trickle,  R.F.C.  1st Violin.
        C.Q.M.S. J. McVie,    R.Scots.2nd Violin.
        Sergt. Tove,          A.O.C.  Clarionette.
        1st/AM.D.Hanson.      R.F.C.  'Cello.
                              ───
        Managing Director.............S.S.M.T.Pollock,ASC.
        Stage Settings by Spr.R.S.Barber & Cpl.A.Admans.
            Scenery painted by A.M's  Hearne and Lea,
                                    3rd A.A.P..
```

When death smiles all you can do is smile back and hold a concert party. This programme was treasured by soldier Samuel Wrigglesworth of Coventry in memory of a precious night of frivolity amidst the gloom. (Courtesy Alan Wrigglesworth)

THE WIPERS TIMES

In early 1916, soldiers of 12th Battalion Sherwood Foresters stumbled on an abandoned printing press in a bombed out house in Belgium, an enterprising sergeant printing a sample page of a pilot publication launched as *The Wipers Times* (in reference to the soldiers' pronunciation of Ypres). Published between February 1916 and February 1918, the satirical journal was stuffed with irreverent poems, lampoons and wry jokes, gallows humour infusing ever page:

BUILDING LAND FOR SALE
BUILD THAT HOUSE ON HILL 60
BRIGHT – BREEZY & INVIGORATING

COMMANDS AN EXCELLENT VIEW
OF HISTORIC TOWN OF YPRES
FOR PARTICULARS OF SALE CONTACT BOSCH & CO MENIN

*

SITUATIONS VACANT: FEW WIRE CUTTERS – good openings
for sharp young men – Apply BOX 203 No Man's Land

*

WEATHER FORECAST
5 to 1 mist
11 to 2 east wind or front
8 to 1 chlorine

SWEETS, RATS AND RAIN

'The peppermints in the parcel were very nice but now the weather is warmer and we are not in the trenches, I don't think you should send them again. Some other really nice sweets would be very welcome. Does the 7lb limit still apply? I have an idea that they had raised it to 11lb again?'

'The rats everywhere were worse than I have ever experienced. Any amount of fellows had their haversacks half chewed up. The rats greatest feat was to kill and devour five kittens nearly three weeks old that the trench cat was rearing in one of the dugouts.'

'It had rained all day & it rained all night. I slept in a puddle with the rain coming in on me, but slept nevertheless. Many prisoners have been taken here.'

(Extracts from April, June and July letters sent by Second Lieutenant Roland Mountfort to his mother in Coventry.)

VIEWS OF NO MAN'S LAND

'Fine weather, intermittent shelling of our trenches throughout the day – 2 killed and 1 slightly wounded. Many wounded seen in 'NO MAN'S LAND' making efforts to return.'

Sam and a comrade posing in a trench. (Courtesy Alan Wrigglesworth)

(2 July extract from a 1st/7th Territorial Battalion Royal Warwickshire Regiment officer's daily Somme report.)

(The shelling badly injured Samuel Wrigglesworth of Hillfields, Coventry in the leg and he would spend the next two years in a Devonport Hospital.)

OPENING TIME

'I went to the knocking shop. They were great big women, most of them, and they were all sitting round a big table waiting for opening time. When I came in 'Ah!' The blue-eyed garcon! Ici! I was so embarrassed by the time I got to the bedroom I couldn't get a stand at all. I was – what do you call it? – impotent. It was the first time I'd had that sort of woman. We'd heard all these tales of disease and I was a bit apprehensive. But I went once or twice afterwards and it was all right. She'd be wearing a thin kimono to give you the feeling straightaway and she fleeced you for about ten francs. I picked the youngest one every time and it was all very quick. In and out.'

(Anonymous. Local brothels *The Fancies, The Poplar Tree* and *Plug Street* were regularly advertised in the *Wipers Times*.)

DEATH OF A CRICKETING LEGEND

On 22 July 1916, Private Percy Jeeves of the 15th Battalion Royal Warwickshire Regiment was killed at High Wood, Montauban in France. In his fiftieth and final first class match, outstanding cricketer Jeeves bowled his Warwickshire side to victory over the champions Surrey in September 1914.

Snatched from obscurity by Bears secretary RV Ryder whilst on holiday in Wensleydale in North Yorkshire, the modest all-rounder Tyke went on, from 1912 to 1914, to humble the greats of the Golden Age of cricket, hitting Wilfred Rhodes for six, bowling Jack Hobbs and outclassing Plum Warner, the England captain.

Percy Jeeves's body was never found but he is remembered on the Thiepval Memorial and in the cricketing hall of fame as an outstanding talent who would have played for England. He is also remembered for becoming a literary icon.

On 14 August 1913, Gloucestershire were playing Warwickshire in Cheltenham. In the crowd was an admiring P.G. Wodehouse, who was captivated by the style of the young Yorkshireman. 'Jeeves must have impressed me,' he confided three years later, 'for I remembered him when I was in New York starting the Jeeves and Bertie saga. It was just the name I wanted. I remember admiring his action very much.'

INTERNATIONAL COMMUNITY AGHAST AT GERMAN BARBARITY... AGAIN

In the month of July, yet another savage killing of a civilian by the German army galvanised world opinion. On 27 July, Captain Charles Fryatt of the merchant navy was executed by firing squad for attempting to ram a German U-boat in 1915.

Fryatt had four skirmishes with German submarines. On 3 March 1915, as skipper of the SS *Wrexham*, he was attacked and chased for forty nautical miles to Rotterdam. He bravely refused to be cowed and ordered his vessel to utilise every puff of steam, his ship limping into port with charred funnels. Later that month, he was waylaid aboard SS *Colchester*, again managing to escape. On 28 March came his third confrontation. His ship, SS *Brussels,* was ordered to stop by the captain of U33 prior to its sinking by torpedo. In accordance with Admiralty rules, which stated that U-boats should be attacked, Fryatt ordered full steam ahead in an attempt to ram the vessel. It promptly crash dived. On 25 June 1916, SS *Brussels* set sail from Holland under cover of darkness for Harwich, five German destroyers ambushing the ship and taking Fryatt prisoner. He was court martialed and found guilty of being a *franc-tireur* (a free-shooter or resistance fighter).

An execution notice was published in Dutch, French and German. It read:

NOTICE

The English captain of a merchant ship, Charles Fryatt of Southampton, though he did not belong to the armed forces of the enemy, attempted on March 28 1915 to destroy a German submarine by ramming it down. For this he has been condemned to death by judgement this day of the Field Court Marshall of the Naval Corps and has been executed. A ruthless deed had been thus avenged belatedly but justly.

Signed: Von Schröder, Admiral Commandant of the Naval Corps, Bruges, July 27 1916.

International condemnation of the brutality was expressed by journalists the world over. The *New York Herald* proclaimed that the execution was: 'The crowning German atrocity. Switzerland's *Journal de Genève* noted: 'It is monstrous to maintain that armed forces have a right to murder civilians but that civilians are guilty of a crime in defending themselves.'

Paying them back in spades. (www.gwpda.org/photos)

GERMANY'S GLOBAL AMBITIONS

'A central News message from Rome says: The *Giornale d'Italia* learns that the most popular book in Germany just now is one by Otto Richard Tannenberg, entitled *Gross Deutschland* which, in spite of the chastening experiences of the last two years, takes an amazingly Utopian view of Germany's future.

'The book lays down an astonishing programme of German expansion in Asia, Africa, South America and Polynesia. Among the future conquests to be achieved by German might, the author includes the whole of Asia Minor, Syria, Palestine, Mesopotamia, Northern Arabia, China, the Congo, Madagascar, Morocco, and the whole of South America as far as the River Amazon. Moreover, he has a vision of all the Dutch colonies becoming German possessions.

'For Austria, Herr Tannenberg predicts a wonderful transformation, calmly assigning to it Poland, Roumania, Serbia, Bulgaria, Montenegro, Albania and Macedonia.

'But even this is not all. Germany, he says, will gain nine Russian provinces, having an area of 120,000 square kilometres, besides which Russia will have to pay an indemnity of fifty milliards of marks. Germany's world empire over and above her present territory, according to Herr Tannenberg, will comprise 22,831,871 square kilometres with a population of 136,563,915.' (Feature in the *Kenilworth Advertiser* 12 August.)

BANK HOLIDAY POSTPONED

In a plea to the nation, General Haig exhorted factory workers to maintain their output of munitions during August to keep the guns blazing. Acknowledging the call from the front, the Government decided to postpone the bank holiday. Workers on the production lines grimaced and bore it although the *Coventry Graphic* painted a more patriotic picture:

'The Premier's appeal had not fallen on deaf ears. The holiday will be willingly, nay gladly, surrendered in order that the attack

The Big Push. 'Well, I'm not taking a holiday myself just yet but I'm sending these kids of mine for a little trip on the continent.' (LMA)

so brilliantly begun may be carried to a victorious conclusion. The Coventry munitions workers, although wearied with long hours of arduous toil, will continue to give of their best, buoyed up in the knowledge that the holidays will be given in full as soon as the military exingencies permit.'

QUEST FOR GOLD THWARTED
Following qualification for the Olympics, international swimmer Rose Sadler, of Stanley Road Coventry, had her high hopes of winning a gold medal dashed following the cancellation of the Games. In her long career she amassed an impressive twenty three medals.

COVENTRY UNITED
'So, within the last eighteen or twenty years, the working men of Coventry have been inured to the tremendous strains being put upon them. Today, therefore, you will find men working from six in the morning till nine every night every day in the week, including Sundays, month after month and never thinking of a rest. Since the war began, the factory whistles are heard on Sunday mornings just the same as on weekdays. The clergy are setting a splendid example. Canon Baille, the head of the Chapter of St Michael's Collegiate Church, whilst unable to make shells, has been working in the hayfield to release a man who can. Go into the municipal tramcar sheds and you will find Canon Simpson engaged in the humble occupation of washing tramcars to relieve a man who has joined the army. Wander into one of the munition works and you will come across the Reverend Arthur Wood, a local Primitive Methodist minister, engaged in turning shells. Men engaged in sedentary office work have thrown up their jobs and donned the blue overalls of the ordinary workman. Orders came from the War Office and the Admiralty for hundred of thousand of shells, and as more men were wanted, the local Socialist party invaded the music halls and the cinema shows, delivering stirring addresses and succeeding in securing two thousand more workers.

'Of course the women of Coventry did not allow themselves to be left out. If ministers of religion could turn shells, they, at any rate, could prepare fuses. If local pastors could drive tramcars, the women could act as conductors. If young men left their clerks' stools there were plenty of young women prepared to take their places. The Mayoress, Miss Doris Pridmore, takes round the laundry work of a local firm, whilst a girl friend of hers drives the horse, thus releasing two men to make munitions, and they both give their earnings to the Wounded Soldiers' Fund.

Messrs Hillman recently advertised that they could provide work for some women and the next morning they had 340 applications. A war work depot for elderly women was established and crowds of them are now busy making canvas goods.

'The town is in real earnest. Wonderful is the quickness with which people who never had before in their lives been within factory gates have learned what is required of them. With no nonsense about playing at munition manufacture or yielding to petty squabbles about precedence and notoriety, the masses go to their work at six o'clock in the morning and, with brief intervals for food, remain till six, seven or nine o'clock in the evening.

'The town is legitimately proud of what it is accomplishing. Yet it may be said that the chief pride is in those homes which have sent sons to the fighting line. There is a sort of rivalry amongst families as to which can boast of having most sons at the front. When a soldier is wounded or pays the greatest price of all, there is further pride in the knowledge that the men have suffered or have died for their country. Here is a little story which indicates the sentiment of the place. There were two workmen who went on a spree for a few days. When they returned to work, they were called before the manager, who pointed out to them that their absence had meant a deficiency in supply and that probably that deficiency had accounted for the deaths of some of their mates in Flanders. The two men stood and listened, and then, realising their responsibilities, they both burst into tears and swore never again would they be remiss. The workmen themselves in one of the great factories have provided a fund out of which they help the dependants of their fellows who are away in the war. The management and clerical staff contribute 2.5% of their income, whilst the ordinary workmen hand over a penny on every pound that they earn, with the result that since last September, up to the end of July, this one firm raised £4,000.

'It can be said that there is not a single able-bodied man in Coventry who, directly or indirectly, is not assisting in the war – a noble record. Indeed, there is such a demand for workers that between four and five hundred Belgians are engaged and special motor-omnibuses are run to Birmingham, Warwick, Kenilworth and elsewhere for the purpose of bringing in additional hands. The whole place hums with activity. As I went through great sheds where men where fitting up motor ambulances and machine shops where engines for both motors and aeroplanes were being made, and other shops where shells were being manufactured, and when I stood out on the flying field where aeroplanes were being tested, I felt that here was the finest repudiation of the story that sometimes one hears that England is not doing her share.' (September article in the *Coventry Standard.*)

WHITE AND POPPE VISIT

'A party of us were shown round White and Poppe's Munition Works at Coventry. About 5,000 women are employed there. The rooms are extremely well ventilated. Of course, there is a strong smell of petrol and a very great and continuous noise from the machinery. We were given passes to the part where high explosives are made and before going into the part we were all given galoshes to put over our own boots so that there might be no danger of our boots causing an explosion.' (September 14 diary entry by Cordelia Leigh.)

Loyal and long serving employees of White and Poppe were presented with badges. (Courtesy Herbert Art Gallery & Museum.)

THE GREEN, GREEN GRASS OF HOME

'We continually hear of the '*Herald*' in the trenches on all fronts. This week, a Coventry naturalist, in expressing the hope that the *Fauna and Flora* column would go on, said the he was fully aware from correspondence he had received in relation to it from officers of the Warwickshire Battalions in Mesopotamia that they regularly interest themselves in it and hoped it would continue.

'Coventry lies in the loveliest country and it might be thought that those inhabitants capable of a new sensation would instinctively make the very best and fullest use of such a favoured situation in the way of learning all that it could teach through its great variety of vegetation, fossils, animals, birds and insects.' (*The Coventry Herald.*)

A CHURCH MADE FROM CINDERS

The urgent need for accommodation to house immigrant munitions workers in the Holbrooks area sparked a hurried construction programme. Many workers were Catholics whose spiritual needs were met by the erection of a new church – St Luke's - constructed from cinder blocks at the junction of Lythalls Lane and Holbrook Lane. Adjacent to the church was a wooden hut used for community activities.

BIG GUNS

'I used to watch the huge naval guns for HMS *Chester*, HMS *Birkenhead* and other warships being turned on massive lathes in the naval shop, which was a quarter of a mile long.'

(Memories of Marguerite Thorn, who began working at the Coventry Ordnance Works as a fourteen year old girl.)

DRAFT DODGERS BEWARE

Coventry's first investigation of men absenting themselves from military service was carried out at the Corn Exchange on 8 October. Under the terms of the Military Service Act, men were summoned to a meeting, police and military officials examining papers and making one arrest. The names and addresses of attendees not having papers were recorded for later investigation.

THE HARPIES OF COVENTRY

On 16 October an article entitled 'Munitions Workers and Bad Housing' was published in a London newspaper, claiming that Coventry was swamped by 240,000 lodgers over and above the original population. The writer deplored the condition of the housing stock and labelled the incomers as 'The Harpies of Coventry'.

FROM THE FIGHTING LINE TO COVENTRY

'The convoy of one hundred wounded and sick who arrived in Coventry on Sunday and are now the guests of the city at the local hospital, came straight from France and most of them were in the recent fighting. Forty of the men were able to walk; the other sixty were stretcher cases. They looked tired and were necessarily travel stained, bearing impress of strain and fatigue. But they were cheerful, smiling brightly all the time when conversed with. It was a spectacle that stirred, though there was no show, no colour, not even warmth and sunshine and one that however often repeated could never fail of appeal – the thought that these were some of the many gallant men whose deeds and devotion in the noblest of causes have made the name of England resound throughout the civilised world as it never before in its battle history; some of the men who were helping to save liberty for the world from the attack of a most horrible foe.

'The train arrived from an English port at 3.56 pm and was met by a fleet of Red Cross ambulances and private motorcars. Refreshments were served out to the men among whom several visitors distributed cigarettes and matches. Those unable to walk left first; then the cot cases were lifted out and placed on the platform pending their transfer to waiting vehicles. Few were too ill but were able to smoke, though the cigarette had to be placed in their mouths and the match lit for them. If anyone yet has not rendered this meed of admiration for the British soldier, has not yet shed the artificialities which prevent the play of natural emotion, the sight of such helplessness, so manfully and quietly borne, could not fail both to reveal and to move.

'It was a busy three quarters or so of an hour. But there was no bustle, no noise, everything being done with marked efficiency and expedition. Coventry City VAD assisted by some members of the St John Ambulance Association undertook the clearing arrangements. A crowd of people watched the evacuation of the train and sympathetically greeted the heroes as they were driven past.

'By 4.40 pm the last patient had been allocated to his bed. The patients bore their suffering bravely and with great cheer, their sense of thankfulness at the end of their long journey being apparent.

'There are now 138 soldiers in the hospital, most of the earlier convoy of wounded men having left the institution before Sunday. While it is not easy to maintain interest in anything on the highest plane, this is an occasion when the Coventry public should see in what directions they could do even more than they are doing for the hospital. No doubt there are many, for a large place like that necessarily wants plenty of things besides money. The city never gave hospitality to more honoured guests and the utmost that is done for them is little compared with what they have done for the city.' (*The Coventry Herald.*)

DEATH WISH

'In November 1917, we were marching towards Hermies and whilst bivouacking we encountered our first shellfire. I must say I felt very envious of one or two of our fellows who were carried away slightly wounded, knowing they were not going into action. I was really frightened to death and I would have given anything to have been killed or wounded.

'The following day, we were issued with further ammunition and mills grenades and took up positions in the trenches. Later that night I had the experience of 'going over the top'. I would have given anything to have missed that terrible ordeal. I was certainly frightened out of my wits, and, upon reflection, feel that I must have been a coward.' (Recollections of Eric Jordan of Humber Avenue, Coventry.)

JAUNDICED JACK

'A dolorous description of a dismal, dusty dugout, designed to describe the deadly denizens of this disgusting district. Time, 2.30 pm, April 17 1916. Lunch just disposed of and I sit in my dugout, a narrow cell, 6ft long, 2ft 6in wide and 3ft 6in high, carved by apparently very unskilled labour slightly in the rear of our front line trench. My roof is a very worn ground sheet that has endured the vicissitudes of countless campaigns. I lie, not elegantly clad in worn out boots, puttees, shorts and shirt. There are also occasional clouds of dust, as an enemy sniper blazes away in a conscientious endeavour to spoil my temper and waste his Government's SAA, in both of which charitable endeavours he may succeed. Zip-brr! There he goes again. My outlook though not classical is rugged in outline and consists of the opposite wall of the communication trench and a pile of earth on which repose sundry articles of attire, discarded for greater comfort by my trusty valet. I forgot to mention that I am not the only creature for which this dugout was constructed, for there are 8,311 vile, vicious, cannibalistic flies, vying one with another to discover some fresh torment for the helpless sufferer. Also three spiders of weird design, one centipede and numerous grasshoppers, locusts, ants and beetles: and in the night watches 'skeeters and sand flies' – and they all love Jack!

'Zip-brr! Damn that sniper!

'On the bank opposite small reptiles sun themselves and in the dried herbage beyond, large lizards and snakes are disporting. Overhead continually pass coveys of the common sand grouse (a very estimable bird; our mess accounted for two yesterday), green starlings, a species of lark and various interesting representatives of the snipe and plover family.

'That sniper! He's at it again.

'Your loving son,

'Jack.'

(Letter from a Coventry officer, sent from Mesopotamia and published in *The Kenilworth Advertiser.*)

CHAPTER 4

1917:
Over There

 Johnny get your gun, get your gun, get your gun,
Take it on the run, on the run, on the run.
Hear them calling you and me,
Every son of liberty.

Hurry right away, no delay, no delay, go today,
Make you daddy glad to have had such a lad.
Tell your sweetheart not to pine,
To be proud her boy's in line.

Over there, over there,
Send the word, over there,
That the Yanks are coming, the Yanks are coming,
The drums rum-tumming everywhere.

So prepare a prayer,
Send the word, send the word to beware,
We'll be over, we're coming over,
And we won't be back till it's over, over there.

DIG FOR VICTORY
On 15 January, the Small Holding and Allotments Committee of Coventry City Council approved a scheme offering free 1/8th acre allotments to local residents. Gardeners had to agree to cultivate the land and offer all produce for sale to benefit city charities.

TRAIN DERAILMENT ON CITY BOUNDARY
In the last week of January, the 9.25 pm Coventry to Kenilworth
passenger train collided in the dark with a stationary goods train on the
outskirts of the city. The goods train was badly damaged and one
waggon was derailed but there were only minor injuries to passengers.

DAY TRIPPERS BESIEGE CASTLE
Taking advantage of a rare Whitsuntide break from their factories,
workers headed for the open fields and castle of nearby Kenilworth.
Such was the press of passengers on the trains that hundreds decided
to walk, the mass of people clearing all baker and teashop shelves by
midday. Unable to accommodate the demand for return tickets, the
Coventry station master ordered that no more were to be sold after 2
pm, forcing many disappointed holidaymakers to walk home or find
beds in Kenilworth.

HOW MUCH!
Coventry and District Licensed Victuallers Association responded to
the government's restrictions on the output of beer and deliveries from
bonded wine and spirit stores with a stark announcement of price
increases. From 2 April, the charges were to be as follows:

> Mild and bitter ales and stout – glass 2½d, half pint 3½d, pint 7d.
> Bottled Bass, Worthington and Guinness – half pint 6d, reputed
> pint 9d, imperial pint 1s.
> Whiskies per glass – 6½d and 7d.
> Brandy 8d (one star), 10d (three star).

(Coventry was awash with pubs! A 1912 survey revealed an astonishing
637 licensed establishments across the city, not counting hotels. There
were eight pubs on the short Park Street alone. Edwardian music hall
act Harry Dale from Birmingham, who died in 1914, eulogised about
the over abundance of drinking dens in Coventry, poetically listing 140
in his famous forty-four-line monologue *The Drinker's Dream.)*

THE HORRORS OF WAR
> 'The local public were seemingly inclined to regard the
> announcement on Monday that beer was to be increased in price

in Coventry by a half penny per glass as one of the most striking illustrations of the horrors of war that had been brought to their notice for some time. As a topic of conversation that evening, it shouldered the other war news of the day into the background and newsagents generally were noticed to be giving preference to the beer price contents poster of our evening paper. Even the little gamins who retail the paper in the streets showed their usual unerring instinct as to relative news values. I overheard a couple of them debating the contents of a handbill in Greyfriars Lane that evening. 'What's on it, kid?' said one and the other read out; 'Fury of Verdun Battle – Germans' Terrible Losses.' There was a moment's grave deliberation and then the first one said with firm decision: 'I shall shout 'Beer's Gone Up!' At that moment both youngsters had uplifted their voices and were striking dismay into the hearts of the populace with grave intelligence.' (*Coventry Graphic.*)

WHERE'S THE MEAT?
In April, patrons of Coventry restaurants found themselves subject to compulsory rationing on many of the more popular dishes as a consequence of the newly enacted Public Meals Order. Diners at boarding houses, clubs and hotels were also affected, gourmets having to contend with meat and potato absent meals and a great reduction in the availability of bread, cakes and pastries.

FOOD MARCH
'In fact, in 1917 in Coventry we had an enormous demonstration against shortages and we carried banners – EQUAL FOOD – EQUAL DISTRIBUTION. This was a veiled threat that if there was not a proper distribution of food there would be trouble, unless there was a proper regard at top levels for the need for reasonable allocations and so on. It was a mass parade with home made banners and slogans and a complete sense of solidarity.'

(Testimony of marcher George Hodgkinson. A system of full rationing for all was introduced in 1918.)

WILL WE STARVE?

Behind the protests were two stark and irrefutable facts that politicians were anxious to hide. In island Britain, three out of every four mouthfuls that sustained the population were dependent on sea-borne food and by the spring of 1917, German U-boats were sinking half a million tons of shipping every month.

THEY WERE ONLY THERE FOR THE MONEY

'They all went yellow. You know, very yellow. And there were quite a lot of them. I don't think they bothered at all. But some of them used to make up decently and cover it up. But I don't think they cared a hang whether they looked yellow or green as long as they got the money – that was all they were interested in. But the majority of them in the loading were all on this TNT. Quite yellow they were.'

(George Ginns a former White & Poppe employee speaking about his female co-workers.)

BLACK POWDER BURNT HER THROAT AWAY

'She went to the doctor and the doctor said she was under the influence of alcohol because she was falling about and she couldn't hold herself up. So the doctor told her to come back when she was sober. Well, I went down to the doctor and I said to him 'She doesn't drink.' He said, 'I think she's under the influence of drink.' And I said she wasn't. 'There's something wrong with her because she's falling about all the time.' And, of course, she was only 19 – she died before she was 20. They took her to hospital. She died in terrible pain and they said that they reckoned the black powder burnt the back of her throat away.'

(Lilian Miles recalling the tragic death of her sister Grace. Both women came to work in a Coventry munitions factory in 1917.)

A POSITIVE PUBLIC DANGER

Such was the appalling rate of battlefield casualties on the Western Front and elsewhere that recruiting agencies across the country trawled ever deeper in enlisting more men. Candidates previously rejected on the grounds of physical infirmity or poor health were recalled for new assessments and men exempted because their skills had once been deemed vital to the war effort were recalled for interview. Even doctors were not exempt. At a meeting of the Coventry Insurance Committee on April 30, an alarmed Surgeon Major Orton reported that eleven local doctors had received formal notice of call up. He stressed that if these men were drafted, the whole medical system in the city would be devastated. He warned that he could not provide for the medical needs of the area, especially in view of the large increase in population brought about by the influx of munitions workers. The committee fully endorsed the views of the Surgeon Major and adopted a resolution to be conveyed to the proper quarters stressing that 'it would be a positive public danger to still further deplete the number of medical men in the crowded area of the city of Coventry'.

THE STRONG CARRIES SAFETY

On 6 July, HMS *Coventry* was launched, entering service in the Baltic Sea with the 5th Light Cruiser Squadron in February 1918. After May 1919, the vessel became the HQ in German waters for the Inter-Allied Disarmament Commission set up under the terms of the Treaty of Versailles to disarm Germany and restrict the capacity for waging war at sea by any nation. The noble, if ultimately unrealistic aim of the commission, was to limit each country's capacity for waging war to levels consistent with the preservation of national security, thus ensuring that defeated Germany and all the great powers would never again have the wherewithal to repeat the horrors of the Great War.

HMS *Coventry.* (Courtesy Herbert Art Gallery & Museum)

Badge of HMS Coventry - image 16 in the Will's Cigarettes Ships' Badges series of 50 cards. The reverse notation is: 'LIGHT CRUISER 2,190 TONS. Guns: 5-6 inch, 2-3 inch. A.A. Badge: The Arms of the City of Coventry. Present ship launched 6th July 1917.'(LMA)

The grave of royal marine Charles Cleaver Yates in the London Road Cemetery. (LMA)

Curiously, the discussions aboard HMS *Coventry* (see ITN Source newsreel footage on the Internet showing delegates posing on the warship's deck off Heligoland in 1920) prefigure Coventry's peace and reconciliation initiative after World War Two by nearly three decades.

HMS *Coventry* saw distinguished service during the Second World War. She was sunk after being torpedoed by an Italian submarine in the Mediterranean on 14 September 1942. Her motto? *Fortis Fert Securitatem – The Strong Carries Safety.*

THE YANKS HAVE COME

On the 18 May, the first contingent of American soldiers reached the UK, the appetite for war diminishing with every new recruit. In France, there was a growing number of desertions, particularly by French troops and on 3 June a well attended and widely reported anti-war meeting was held in Leeds, Siegfried Sassoon capturing the national mood of mounting hopelessness in a searing poem about a soldier fortifying his trench:

> He pushed another bag along the top,
> Craning his body outward, then a flare,
> Gave one white glimpse of No Man's Land and wire,
> And as he dropped his head, the instant split,
> His startled life with lead and all went out.

VANGUARD SUNK

On the evening of 9 July, a massive explosion on board HMS *Vanguard* sent the aged vessel to the bottom of the harbour in Scapa Flow in the Orkney Islands, 801 seamen drowning within a few minutes. One crew member, former King Henry VIII school pupil Edward Leslie Peirson, had stayed aboard to catch up with work as his fellow officers left to attend a party, his German connections suggesting a sinister intent. Leaving school in 1905, Peirson continued his education at Heidelberg College in Germany, the *Kenilworth Advertiser* in a suggestive article in November 1914, referring to his absence as receiving 'special instruction in the enemy's country'. The seeds of doubt were sown and a hurriedly convened Court of Enquiry considered the deceased's action, noting: 'There was also found a German Bible, bearing the name of Assistant Paymaster, RNV, E.L. Peirson (the name as spelt, being German), one of the officers of the Vanguard who was lost with the ship; and also a letter, written in German, without address, introduction or signature, the contents of which might be considered most incriminating.' No further light was shed on these contents, the Admiralty concluding that the ship was lost as a consequence of an accident involving the magazine. The tragedy overshadowed Peirson's exemplary service as Gunnery Officer and Head of the Plotting Table on board *Vanguard* at the Battle of Jutland on 31 May 1916. The body of one of the founder members of the King Henry VIII's 'Old Boys Club' was never recovered.

A TRAGIC ACCIDENT IN TRAINING
In July, former *Triumph* employee Private Ernest Ball of the Royal Warwickshire Regiment died of his wounds in Ranelagh Road Military Hospital in Ipswich after an accident during bayonet practice.

HOW TO FLY
He solved at last the secret
Of swift dynamic flight
By rising to the heavens
Upon some dynamite!

L. C. Ball

Trench art. If you were to survive you needed a good sense of humour! (Courtesy Pat Warren).

PASSCHENDAELE

In three and a half hellish months, beginning on 31 July, British troops advanced just five thousand yards over Flemish mud. The loss of life was heavier than the combined losses sustained in conquering India and Canada a century and a half earlier.

BUT WE WILL KEEP OUR PECKERS UP

'‘Eh corporal what's this?’ asked the soldier examining his meagre breakfast.

'That, my lad, is your bread ration.’

'Blimey! A thowt it were ‘oly Communion!’

HOUSEKEEPING IN WARTIME

'At the beginning of the year when Lord Devenport's rations for bread, sugar and meat were announced, I found great difficulty in keeping within the allowance. As I tried to use substitutes for meat and bread, the price of those substitutes rose, because, I suppose, so many more people were buying them too. I have a family of six to provide for. I first thought that if I allowed ten loaves a week and three pounds of flour, I should be able to feed the children well and allow enough flour for making cakes and an occasional pudding with flour. I found that I did not use quite ten loaves a week and I needed a little more flour for cooking. During last week, I arranged two kinds of breakfast for alternate days. On Monday we each had a plate of porridge with milk. I cut 12 2oz slices of bread, which allowed two pieces per person. We had either jam or butter with our bread. I see that Lord Devenport has been urging people who can afford it to eat more meat and leave bread for the poorer people. All the meat, bones and gristle I put into a pot and boil well, adding any meat remains during the week and this makes a good gravy for the meat and with soup thickening makes a most delicious soup.

'The sugar allowance for each person is half a pound; this

amount, when there are several children in the house is not very much but so far I have kept within our allowance. I and my husband have given it up some time ago. I never put sugar on the table as children generally want it if they see it before them.

'I find that milk is a very heavy expense but, so far, I have not found a substitute. I take about two quarts each day.

'During my experience of housekeeping in wartime I find that with a little ingenuity and careful thinking and planning, it is quite possible to keep within rations.'

(Upper V schoolmistress writing in the July edition of Barr's Hill School Magazine.)

EVERY BERRY AND FIBRE COUNTS

In August, recognising that every morsel of food was vital to the war effort, the Food Production Department and the Board of Education collaborated in devising a national plan to harvest the nation's blackberry crop. With time off from classes, schoolchildren were encouraged to forage in the local hedgerows to collect berries for jam making and were paid one penny per pound for their efforts.

In Coventry, youngsters were persuaded to be even more adventurous by a local reporter. 'The hedges of the countryside around Coventry yield more than one harvest,' he suggested. 'Just now we are reminded that they are yielding a harvest that is usually neglected but which by reason of the war has come to have national value. It is a harvest … of wool!' Children were asked to gather fibres of wool from bramble bushes and barbed wire fences and to collect residues from the process of shearing. 'And now you've collected it, get knitting!'

LETTERS BY THE SACKFUL … AND GRIM RESOLUTION

By August, some 1.1 million letters and parcels were being sent to the Western Front every day, some enclosing precious photographs, locks of hair, good luck charms, soap and sweets. In forlorn return, many correspondents endured an unremitting silence, only the angels of death dressed as telegram boys tapping on random knockers. Some women in Coventry trembled as they opened their doors and received envelopes from the military, many collapsing on reading dreadful news. There were stories elsewhere of women slitting their throats in anguish

Thousands of embroidered greetings cards like this were sent from the front. (Courtesy Pat Warren)

but most people, like their loved ones in the trenches, grinned and bore the pain. An American diplomat summed up the resolution of those who worked and waited in the following words:

'How to pull the English off, that's a hard thing to say, as it is a hard thing to say how to pull a bulldog off. Not a tear have I seen yet. They take it as part of greatness and of empire. You guess at their grief only by their reticence. They use as few words as possible and then courteously take themselves away. It isn't an accident that these people own a fifth of the world. Utterly unwarlike, they outlast everybody else when war comes. You don't get a sense of fighting here, only of endurance and of high resolve. The nation is sad, dead earnest, resolute and united: not a dissenting voice – silent. It will spend all its treasure and give all its men if need be. I have never seen such grim resolution.'

QUEEN VISITS WHITE AND POPPE ON 18 SEPTEMBER

'The reception at the factory was one that the royal visitors will long remember. A large proportion of the employees are girls and women and their greeting was unmistakably hearty. It took the combined efforts of a number of special constables who joined hands to keep back the excited young ladies who pressed forward so vehemently. At one of the principle entrances was displayed a floral archway with the word 'WELCOME' designed in blooms. Here Her Majesty was presented with a bouquet of roses by the woman worker with the longest record of service in the tetryl rooms. During the tour, over 10,000 employees were seen at their respective tasks. It was interesting to observe that the royal party were called upon to comply with all the regulations framed for the purpose of safety. The male members of the party handed over to the works police such articles as matches, pipes, cigars and cigarettes. At one point in the procession, the works' fire brigade were drawn up. They were in uniform with hatchets presented and the royal party passed between the lines after a short and interesting interruption. To her majesty was presented a fireman who had distinguished himself by an act of bravery. The particular deed was the carrying for 20 yards of a pail of burning detonators to a place of safety. At another point, she spoke kindly to a worker who had been rendered totally blind by an explosion.' (*Coventry Graphic.*)

DREADFUL ACCIDENTS

'We have two Welsh girls living with us now and nearly everyone around us seems to have girl lodgers. The younger of the girls, Maggie, gets £2 18s a week and she is only 16. There have been a dreadful lot of accidents at W & P lately. Only this morning, the magazine caught fire and we all sat here in the office waiting to be blown up. The girls were running down the lane for dear life in their overalls. On Wednesday, a girl got her arm and half her face blown off. She died yesterday.' (Mrs Ashmore.)

SOLDIERS PARCELS CAMPAIGN

For several weeks, the congregation at the Warwick Road Church donated funds for the purchase of personal items to send to front line troops. Packages were assembled containing tobacco, cigars, shaving sticks, lead pencils, stationery and brown paper, a later appeal collecting eggs for wounded soldiers.

COVENTRY MAN WINS VC

'On 4 October 1917, the 48th Division were in the vicinity of St Julien and the 7th Battalion had as their objective a location known as Tweed House. A Company captured their first objective but when they continued their advance all the officers and non-commissioned officers in Private Hutt's platoon were hit. Private Hutt thereupon took command and led forward the platoon. He was held up at a strong point on his right, but immediately ran forward alone, shot the officer and three men in the post and caused forty or fifty others to surrender. Presently, realising that he had pushed too far ahead, Hutt withdrew his party.'

(Victoria Cross citation recording the gallantry of Arthur Hutt from Caludon Road in Coventry.)

'Sir – It is intended that Corporal Hutt VC shall on his return to his native city be accorded a welcome worthy of his valiant deeds. The citizens will, I am sure, heartily approve of this, and give it their warmest support. The committee having charge of the arrangements consider, however, that the citizens would desire to give him some tangible proof of their appreciation of his noble and heroic action, which has earned for him the greatest honour for valour which his King and Country can confer. It has accordingly been decided to establish a Fund, the proceeds of which shall be invested in War Stock and presented to him.'

(Letter written by Coventry Mayor Alick Hill to the *Coventry Graphic* in December.)

EXPENSIVE GUESTS

'One of the supreme lessons taught by the war is that the will of the individual must be subordinated to the good of the community. In a wide sense, no man can do as he pleases if such action is detrimental to others. Above everything, it is necessary to conserve the food resources of the country, a necessity that explains the police court proceeding against farmers who neglect to take measures for ridding their ricks of rats. Every man must take measures to ensure that the rat population of his premises is kept down to the lowest possible limits. The country cannot afford hospitality to such expensive guests.' (*The Journal.*)

STRIKE!

Following severe food shortages, stewards led 10,000 male and female employees of White and Poppe on a city wide protest march on 17 and 18 November. By 26 November, the entire workforce of the premier munitions manufacturer in the country had gone on strike, 50,000 angry and disgruntled employees thronging the streets in a show of strength over shop steward recognition. The strike provoked widespread local and national anger against a backdrop of grave news from the trenches, every newspaper headlining the casualty figures: 'FOUR THOUSAND A WEEK'. Coventry readers sent ugly letters to local newspapers. 'Those who did not agree with the strike should send the addresses of the strike leaders to the men coming home on leave and suggest they call on them', wrote one anonymous reader. 'The military casualty lists should be published side by side with the strike news', thundered another. Both the *Birmingham Post* and the *Midland Daily Telegraph* recognised the gravity of the situation, many commentators suggesting that the cataclysmic events in revolutionary Russia might, with only minimum provocation, be replicated in a fragmenting Britain. Rumour and intrigue were rife in the thronged city, some strikers even suggesting that German agents had infiltrated the trade union movement in a direct attempt at fostering strikes. Comments in *The Aeroplane* were more vituperative and incendiary than most:

> 'Coventrians were in 1897, and still are the most self-satisfied, self-opinionated, self-conceited, self-centred, pigheaded and muddleheaded people in England. Coventry once had the pick of the world's ribbon and watch trades but lost them because she was too stupid to adopt modern machinery and business methods. Coventry had the cycle trade to itself and lost it. Coventry had the motor trade first and let the cream of it go.

Coventry was the first place to make aeroplane engines but let the trade go to Bristol and elsewhere. These strikers are not after any more money but the recognition of a principle. The idea of Coventry having any principles except money-grubbing is really funny. Strikers in the aircraft factories should be run straight into the army. A shop steward does not carry any weight in the trenches except the weight of his pack. Let them try how they like trench work at a shilling a day. A chaplain has flown back from the Front to preach to Coventry about it. One might as well preach to the self-confident Hun in the frontline trenches. So long as Coventry has a sufficiency of food, alcohol and women it is not going to listen to preaching.' And the final insult to the genuinely aggrieved strikers: 'If shooting was good enough for the Irish rebels, why is it not good enough for English traitors?'

Every day the factories were idle, the strike attracted an ever-mounting tide of bitterness, invective and animosity a letter published in the *Midland Daily Telegraph* on the 29 November from a correspondent signed 'Loyalist' further fanning the flames:

'Sir, I witnessed a demonstration at the gate of Coventry Ordnance Factory this evening and I can safely state that at least fifty per cent of this crowd were young chaps of military age between 19 and 27 years old who were causing all the commotion. Why? Simply because a few girls realised the necessity of delivery the goods and being loyal to both King and country, also to the lads out there facing death for such people as these strikers – or perhaps I should have said slackers – who fail to realise what a shortage of munitions may mean to these gallant lads. I think a lot of these young fellows would be better employed in the Army harassing the Huns instead of these true loyal girls. It would have done the slackers good to have heard the opinion of one of the Warwicks who also witnessed the demonstration. He said he wished the Warwicks had been there and that these slackers would have had a rough five minutes, only he expressed himself a bit more forcibly than I dare write here. Home workers, realise your duty to your kith and kin by helping to keep the output of munitions going.'

A further letter in the same newspaper signed 'Tommies in Hospital' cranked up the disgust even further:

> 'The strike makes us more sick than anything we have gone through in three years of active service. We are bearing all the accidents of war for our one shilling a day while they enjoy their good wages. Do they deserve the name of men?'

Even closer to home, Coventry Mayor Alick Hill joined in the chorus for a return to work with an appeal in the *Birmingham Post,* emphasizing that differences at home should not be allowed to swell the numbers of fallen comrades abroad.

> 'Think of these things,' he rallied, 'and help Haig keep up the pressure on the inhuman foe who murdered Nurse Cavell and Captain Fryatt, sank the *Lusitania*, robbed and ravished women and children and is trying to starve us by his unlimited U-boat campaign.'

Thankfully, all parties - the strikers, the Government and the management of White and Poppe - responded to the torrent of criticism about selfishness and intransigence. All sides in the dispute offered concessions and by 5 December the strikers had returned to work.

CONVALESCING SOLDIERS TAKE TEA
In the Christmas period, the pupils of Barr's Hill School for Girls entertained two parties of wounded soldiers. Before tea, songs and carols were sung, a troupe of girls also giving displays of dancing and drill. After taking refreshments, members of the Elocution Class recited poems, the grateful and appreciative soldiers responding with songs and music.

POLICE REPORT
> 'Under the Defence of the Realm Regulations, no person is allowed to keep Homing Pigeons without a permit. Applications for 321 permits were made, but before their issue, enquires were made as to the suitability of the persons by this Department.'

'The experiment of appointing police women has been amply justified by results. The question of increasing the present staff so that the whole of the suburban area can be adequately covered should receive consideration in the immediate future. The work of police women is mainly preventative and the amount of good achieved is considerable.'

(Report of the Police Establishment for the year ended 31 December 1917.)

SAY THAT AGAIN?
During the war, every worker at Cash's weaving factory had one unforgettable experience.

'You had to learn to lip-read,' recalled Mrs Pearson who spent ten years attending the looms. 'It was the noise. I suppose that's why I'm a bit deaf.'

SCHOOLBOYS DO THEIR BIT
Throughout 1917, pupils at Bablake School volunteered to work in the munitions factories of White and Poppe, giving up their vacations to join the thousands of workers on the production lines to help manufacture shell cases. In addition, they worked in the school metal shop – one of the only such educational facilities engineered to the exacting high tolerances required - producing over five thousand shell cases and thirty packing cases.

SILVER LININGS
'The war has simplified life. People have learned to go without, to distinguish between the necessary and the unnecessary. And it is remarkable how, in the nation, which, for a generation, has been multiplying its comforts and even luxuries and satisfying tastes, intellectual and physical, that in earlier times had often to be restrained – it is remarkable how easily, for the moment, these, in most cases, gradually realised pleasures in life have been put aside. When the war is over, the current, substantially healthy mind and body expanding, will resume its flow, and at greater speed, for the public know its refreshment. Not only in the last three years have

joys and recreations been restricted till some of us are scarcely conscious that we ever had them, but in many directions have been disappearances or part disappearances, not directly affecting ourselves, which at least formed part of our daily lives.

'Few perhaps really miss the tramp with his unpleasant aspect and more unpleasant ways, the begging, the singing in the streets, the pitiable spectacle of ill-clad, ill-nourished children taken on the road by their parents, in most cases doubtless to excite sympathy. Yet the vagrant has been a social sore for centuries. In vain has legislation taken a hand; sturdy or miserable he has been a witness in all ages to the never-ending failure of the social system.

'The war has done more than acts of parliament, more than the stern repressive measures of the Tudors towards abolishing vagrancy. There are still roadsters. But we see little of them unless we look for them. They are mostly elderly, for many of the young men of military age who could bear arms are in khaki, a number of them having voluntarily enlisted. When duty calls with a sufficiently imperative voice to whom will it not make a successful appeal? The general demand for labour has also been a factor in keeping or taking men and women off the road. A powerful influence in Warwickshire has been for some years, and is now, the scheme administered by the County Vagrancy Committee: it has done much to diminish the plague in the administrative area. To it Coventry largely owes its immunity from the annoyance of street and house begging. Particularly valuable is the close watch the committee keeps on the women and children who go on tramp.' (*The Coventry Herald.*)

RELUCTANT WAR PENSIONERS
Scores of men returned from the distant war zones suffering appalling injuries that consigned many to a life of suffering and inaction. Generally proud and conscientious, these men were often reluctant to avail themselves of war service pensions, feeling that they would be stigmatised and belittled. A campaign in the local press headlined 'DISABLED COVENTRY SOLDIERS – What Every Man Should Know' sought to dispel all hesitancy and encourage men to come forward:

'The War Pensions Local Committee are not distributing charitable funds but funds provided by the State. Every man disabled by war service has a right to a pension or a gratuity. He has a right to the most careful and effective treatment obtainable FREE. That if he requires an artificial limb it will be supplied and maintained in good order FREE of charge. If disability prevents him from returning to his old trade he will receive FREE training for a new one. Unless a man claims a pension based on his former earnings, no account is taken of his earnings or earning capacity or of the extent to which this may be improved by any training that might be given to him. No permanent pension will be reduced because a man has accepted training. While he is being trained, he will receive additions to his pension for the support of himself and his family. Neither treatment or training will cost him a penny.'

Private Sam Wrigglesworth was awarded a pension. (Courtesy Alan Wrigglesworth)

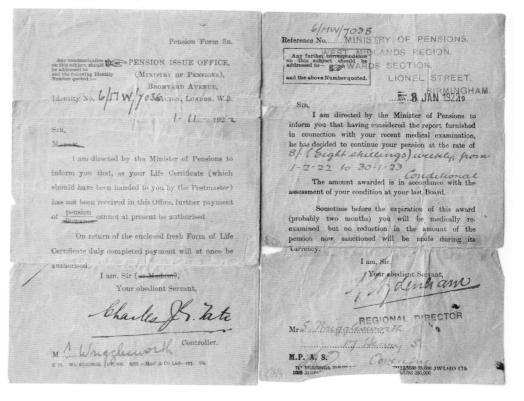

Private Sam Wrigglesworth's service medals. (Courtesy Alan Wrigglesworth)

ROLL UP AND SEE A MOVIE

Elijah Strong, the landlord of the General Wolfe Hotel in Foleshill Road, opened his new Alexandra Picturedrome to great acclaim, bringing silent films to what was a former coffee shop. For a few pennies, customers could forget about the war and watch the latest releases, including the comedies *Poor Little Rich Girl,* starring Mary Pickford and *Coney Island,* featuring Fatty Arbuckle, Buster Keaton and the Keystone Cops. Such was the success of the venture that the cinema soon replaced its piano accompanist with a pit orchestra.

FOOLS GOLD

'Since the beginning of the war, as we know, the belligerent nations have alone issued paper currency in excess of the gold held in reserve to the extent of at least £1,500,000,000 (one thousand five hundred millions). All this new currency or gold substitutes has, in the country of origin, a footing equal to gold so that it is a general fact that the purchasing medium has been increased by at least seventy-five per cent.' (President's address to the Coventry Chamber of Commerce.)

ENCOUNTER WITH THE RED BARON

'I came into contact on two occasions with the Red Baron and his circus but remembering the saying 'He who fights and runs away lives to fight another day,' I cleared out of the way. I was very fortunate in escaping harm from the Baron. I will say, however, that he was a gentleman in every sense of the word – a fine pilot and a clean fighter. He had a knack of keeping at high altitude in the sunlight and then swooping down on unsuspecting enemy aircraft. My machine was on several occasions riddled with bullets and looked like a cullender but fortunately I came home with a whole skin.'

(Flight Lieutenant Ticknell of Albany Road, Coventry remembering his service with 60 Squadron in Belgium. The Red Baron – Manfred von Richthofen – was the war's premier ace with eighty kills. He was shot down, probably by a lone sniper, on 21 April 1918.)

CHAPTER 5

1918:
The Hearse Song

Don't you ever laugh as the hearse goes by,
For you may be the next one to die.
They wrap you up in a big white sheet,
From your head down to your feet.

They put you in a big black box,
And cover you up with dirt and rocks.
All goes well for about a week,
Then your coffin begins to leak.

The worms crawl in, the worms crawl out,
They eat your eyes, they eat your nose,
They eat the jelly between your toes.

A big green worm with rolling eyes,
Crawls in your stomach and out your eyes,
Your stomach turns a slimy green,
And pus pours out like whipping cream.
You spread it on a slice of bread,
And this is what you eat when you are dead. .

THREE AND A HALF MILLION SHELLS
On the 21 March, after a monumental stockpiling of ordnance and munitions, the German forces launched their long planned Spring Offensive against the entrenched British Third and Fifth Armies. Under

a dense blanket of fog, 6,000 heavy guns opened up, delivering salvo after salvo over a 60-mile front. Three and a half million shells rained down on the British positions, the onslaught and the subsequent infantry attack killing and injuring some 200,000 men. German soldiers advanced many miles and took 90,000 prisoners.

NOW WE ARE ALL TOMMIES

Attributing it to nearly four years of constant war, doctors, teachers and parents across the county reported a martial conditioning of children's playtime, nurseries and playgrounds in Coventry echoing to the mimicking cries of war. 'War toys abound,' reported one observer and 'tin kettles are hourly thumped by infants in paper puttees. There is no need to fear that the coming generation will not think war thoughts sufficiently. As one watches them on the floor, one even conceives that their so belligerent imaginations may mature into frightful deeds thereafter. They are our masters since they will rule over the slice of Time that follows us. What will they make of it? May not these war-nourished brains insist upon a period of plunder? May they not decide that war on the whole is more fun? And so make war as an Elizabethan did because peace was so vapid and tasteless?'

'On one side of the floor the other day,' continued the parent, 'we came across a dozen soldiers of wood in various degrees of dismemberment and we were told on no account to touch them as they were dead. We though it right to ask what had killed them? 'Poison gases!' was the answer. And a disused gramophone was pointed out, supposed to be exuding fatal fumes. But wasn't it horrid? Wasn't it rather cruel? No! It was great fun! If grown people will do these things, why not children? It would have been mere hypocrisy to protest and we had to let that and much else of a bloodthirsty sort escape without further contradiction.'

COVENTRY MUNITIONS WORKERS LEAD A NATIONAL
WALKOUT
Responding to the German onslaught in March, the Government
extended the provisions of the Munitions of War Act in an attempt to
recruit yet more conscripts to the Front. The legislation extended the
scope of recruitment to the industrial sector and men up to the age of
23 were to be withdrawn from industry regardless of their occupation.
Factory workers in Coventry were incensed that their protection
afforded by reserved occupation status was to be withdrawn and in late
July they went on strike, despite the lack of formal approval by the
official union. The stoppage encouraged walkouts in Birmingham and
elsewhere and a resolute War Cabinet met to debate the crisis, warning
that unless the strikers returned to work by 29 July they would be
placing themselves outside the munitions industry, rendering
themselves liable to the provisions of the Military Service Act. The
Coventry strikers were vilified in the Press, a cartoon in *Punch* with
the title *Self or Country* showing a sour-faced Coventry worker talking
to a soldier. 'If I was a soldier,' moans the striker, 'and they tried to
shift me to another part of the line just as I was comfortable, I'd down
tools.' 'No you wouldn't,' responds the soldier. 'If you were a soldier
you'd be out to down Huns.' The animosity was cranked up in a
vituperative telegram sent to the Coventry strikers from fellow workers
at the Woolwich Arsenal:

*NOW YOU WILL EARN THE BLESSING OF THE KAISER
AND HIS ARMY OF MURDERERS. STOP.*

After a few days of negotiation the strikers went back to work.

I WISH I'D SQUEEZED THE TRIGGER
There was vicious hand-to-hand fighting on the French battlefield of
Marcoing on 28 September, 27 year old Private Henry Tandey from
Leamington confronting a limping German soldier at gunpoint. He
hesitated, later confiding: 'I took aim but couldn't shoot a wounded
man, so I let him go'. The man was said to be Adolf Hitler.
    The future Chancellor of Germany always remembered his escape
from death and when he became Nazi leader in 1933, so the story goes,
he ordered his staff to trace Tandey after seeing a painting

commissioned in 1925 for the Green Howards' officers mess. Service records were obtained, together with a copy of the painting by Matania depicting the heroic Tandey carrying a wounded comrade to safety in 1914. Hung on a wall at Hitler's retreat in Berchtesgaden, it was proudly shown to Neville Chamberlain in 1938 during his peace mission, his host remarking: 'That man came so near to killing me that I thought I should never see Germany again. Providence saved me such devilishly accurate fire as those English boys were aiming at us.'

After leaving the army, Henry Tandey resided at 22 Cope Street, Coventry and was employed as a security guard at the Triumph, later the Standard Motor Company. The most highly decorated surviving British private of World War One, winning the VC, DCM and MM, it is said that Tandey always regretted not pulling the trigger in 1918, especially after the bombing of Coventry in 1940, when Cope Street was flattened.

Tandey was harshly and insensitively described by the *Daily Telegraph* in 1918 as 'a hero of the old berserk type'. In a later conversation with a reporter from the *Coventry Evening Telegraph,* the man who ran out of chest space for his multiple medals said: 'Somehow, I never thought I'd get killed. During the fighting, I never knew what time it was or even what day it was and I spent two years in the trenches before I was hit.'

Tandey died in Coventry on 20 December 1977. His ashes were scattered in a British cemetery in Marcoing, near Cambrai.

(Much has been made of the sensationalist claims about Tandey and Hitler but the known facts and surviving evidence undermine the veracity of the story. Tandey had no recollections about the events of September 1918 until the story broke in 1938 and it would seem from examining the facts that it was Hitler who promoted the myth once he became Chancellor in 1933. It seems implausible in the confusion and smoke of battle that Hitler would have retained an unforgettable mental imprint of his saviour for two decades. How would he have been able to recognise Tandey from grainy monochrome photographs and an even more insubstantial image in the Matania painting? And why did that one life sustaining moment in his life, a moment that had allegedly burnt itself into his consciousness, not trigger an attempt to discover Tandey before 1933? It would seem that the delusional Chancellor, who was diagnosed as 'a psychopath with symptoms of hysteria' after the war, seized on the opportunity of an association with a national hero to boost his own persona and prestige, attributing his redemption as a sign from heaven of his larger destiny. Many facts about his war experiences were suppressed, altered or inflated to fit the image of man born to avenge Germany and to conquer the world. On 11 November 1918, when a war weary world listened to the clock strike eleven, a disappointed and bitter Adolf Hitler spoke chillingly to his adjutant, Captain Weidemann, and said the following words: 'Every generation needs its own war and I shall take care that this generation gets its war'.')

PRAYING FOR VICTORY
A National Day of Prayer and Intercession was held in Coventry and throughout the UK on 6 January, the King urging congregations to 'pray that we may have the clear-sightedness and strength necessary for the victory of our cause'.

CITY WELCOMES ITS HERO
On Saturday 12 January, Corporal Hutt returned to Coventry, people thronging the city in their thousands to greet him. His neighbours presented him with an inscribed cigarette box and raised a sign across the street, which read: *WELCOME HOME TO OUR VC*.

FOOD RATIONING TIGHTENED
In January, the Ministry of Food recommended a new scheme for local food rationing to reduce queuing and provide fairer allocations of scarce resources. Every customer was to be registered with one shop for particular foodstuffs and barred from shopping elsewhere. And retailers were instructed to divide their stocks fairly and without favour.

WORDS OF WAR
The banter of war enriched the local vocabulary, the worst insult on the streets of Coventry as elsewhere being the use of the word 'German'. When spat out in anger, this stinging appellation caused inevitable fights. Coventry girls acquired the term 'clicking' to describe the striking up of acquaintances with local boys, hundreds of other

words infiltrating the local vernacular. The lexicon is long and colourful – Baby's Head (a meat pudding field ration); Balloon Goes Up; Blotto; Bully Beef; Chit (a piece of paper); Cushy; Dick Shot Off (the Distinguished Service Order, reserved for officers); Fred Karno's Army; Gone West (killed); Jack Johnson (large artillery shell named after a heavyweight boxing champion); Kaput; Old Bean; Posh; Put a Sock in It; Up Against the Wall; Whizz Bang (high velocity shell); Windy (afraid or nervous).

AMPUTEES RE-TAUGHT TO WRITE

The Local Pensions Committee received a recommended booklet explaining the techniques involved in helping amputees to write with their left hands, its author noting: 'The marked progress which the men under my care have made proves to me how valuable this little booklet is. I can recall men who were formerly gardeners, mattress makers, ironmongers and porters and I have daily noticed them improve from copy to copy.'

FATTENING 'EM UP FOR THE FRAY?

It was announced by the government that as from 1 March, boys who would be over 13 but under 18 on that date would be allowed a supplementary ration of 5oz of bacon with bone or the equivalent 'in meats other than butcher's meat'.

PUTTING THEIR BACKS INTO IT

The effect of the extra hour of daylight gained by the operation of the summer time system was very much appreciated by the citizens of Coventry on Easter Sunday and Monday after a very hard winter. Gardeners and allotment holders were out in force in every part of the city and the wielders of spades and forks were to be seen busy from morning until dusk preparing the ground for sowing.

ZEPPLIN RAIDS COVENTRY

A Zeppelin targeted Coventry on 12 April and bombs were dropped on the grounds of Whitley Abbey and on Baginton Sewage Farm. Commenting on the attack in his memoirs some years later, R.G. Coustois, who was a small boy on the date of the raid, wrote:

'I remember looking up at a silver cigar caught in the searchlights; my grandmother pulling me into the house and making me lie down under the kitchen table. Next day we heard that a bomb had dropped on Whitley Common – killing a cow and making a huge crater. So my grandparents paid the pony and trap man from the off-licence in Providence Street and we went to see the damage.'

The Zeppelin passed over Sowe Common in Walsgrave, disturbing the rest of local character Snob Thompson, who rushed from his bed minus his shirt and trousers. Shaking his fist at the monster, he shouted: 'It's always the same. When you want a policeman you can never find one!'

It seems that the Zeppelin took a northwesterly course towards Birmingham, where it was intercepted at a height of 16,000 feet by an aircraft piloted by Lieutenant Cecil Noble-Campbell, flying from his base in Buckminster. The pilot manoeuvred to attack but was completely oblivious to the presence of his comrade, Lieutenant Brown from C Flight, who was at the controls of a second aircraft approaching from the opposite direction. The two aircraft fired their guns and inadvertently shot each other down, both crashing near Radford Aerodrome as the Zeppelin cruised imperiously on, unaware of the action.

Between 1915 and 1918, there were a frightening 112 aircraft crashes in the West Midlands.

CONTROLLING ALIENS
A survey carried out by government officials in Coventry revealed a total of 1316 aliens resident in the city. Very few were from enemy countries, although all nationalities were represented in the figure and Belgian nationals predominated. Every alien was obliged to carry an identity book at all times and every newcomer had to report to the police on arrival. All movements in and out of the city were recorded.

IRISH LASS DOES HER BIT

'I was offered the option of going to Gretna Green or Coventry and I chose the latter. All I knew about Coventry was that they made bicycles there and that Lady Godiva had ridden through the streets naked to relieve the citizens of high taxes. I arrived at Coventry station and there were hundreds of bicycles on the platform.

'I had to find my way from the station to the hostel at Barras Heath off Swan lane. The hostel was built to hold 500 girls. It was quite cosmopolitan, with girls from Scotland, Wales, Belgium, the Channel Islands as well as girls from my homeland and England. The ordnance factory in Red Lane was only a few minutes walk from the hostel and near enough for us to return for our mid-day meals. These were served to us by 'Ladies' from the upper classes who gave their services free as their war effort and we were well looked after by them and by the maids who made our beds and cleaned our bedrooms.

'There was no reason to go out to the town as all our needs were catered for in the hostel, where there were such facilities as a church, an entertainments room, a sewing room and even a shop.

'They gave me a job in the stores where I allocated the materials to those who were making fuses and I continued to work there until the war ended.' (Sarah Watkins.)

WAR BONDS HOLIDAY BONANZA.

'At the visit of the tank 'Ole Bill to Coventry, there was a procession of school children through the town who brought certificates to the tank. Barr's Hill headed the procession and, on their arrival at Grey Friar's Green, the children were drawn up round 'Ole Bill while Mr Bates, assisted by other well known citizens of the Education Committee, opened the tank. Mr Bates was so pleased with the magnificent amount invested by the school that he gave them a half holiday, whereupon there was much cheering.' (July entry in the Barr's Hill School magazine.)

MANNA FROM HEAVEN?

On Sunday 27 October 1918, during a lull in the gunfire, Sapper Charles Constable heard the drone of a light aircraft and looked up, thinking early snow had begun to flutter from the sky above Masnières,

The German People Offers Peace.

The new German democratic government has this programme:

"The will of the people is the highest law."

The German people wants quickly to end the slaughter.

The new German popular government therefore has offered an

Armistice

and has declared itself ready for

Peace

on the basis of justice and reconciliation of nations.

It is the will of the German people that it should live in peace with all peoples, honestly and loyally.

What has the new German popular government done so far to put into practice the will of the people and to prove its good and upright intentions?

a) The new German government has appealed to President Wilson to bring about peace.

It has recognized and accepted all the principles which President Wilson proclaimed as a basis for a general lasting peace of justice among the nations.

b) The new German government has solemnly declared its readiness to **evacuate** Belgium and to restore it.

c) The new German government is ready to come to an honest understanding with France about.

Alsace-Lorraine.

d) The new German government has restricted the **U-boat War.**

No passengers steamers not carrying troops or war material will be attacked in future.

e) The new German government has declared that it will **withdraw all** German troops back over the German frontier.

f) — The new German government has asked the Allied Governments to name commissioners to agree upon the **practical measures of the** evacuation of Belgium and France.

These are the deeds of the new German popular government. Can these be called mere words, or bluff, or propaganda?

Who is to blame, if an armistice is not called now?

Who is to blame if daily thousands of brave soldiers needlessly have to shed their blood and die?

Who is to blame, if the hitherto undestroyed towns and villages of France and Belgium sink in ashes?

Who is to blame, if hundreds of thousands of unhappy women and children are driven from their homes to hunger and freeze?

The German people offers its hand for peace.

The German handbill. (Courtesy Pat Warren)

near Cambrai, in France. But he soon discovered that the white flakes were not the signs of an early winter but thousands of fluttering handbills, the vast majority falling unread into the churned up, muddy craters of No Man's Land to be dissolved amid the filth and the gore. Some lone leaflets drifted into the British trenches and were quickly

Deutscher Sparkassenverband
Kriegsanleihe-Sparkarte

(Vor= und Zuname) _Kanonier Franz August Meißner_

(Dienstgrad) _Gefr._

(Truppenteil) _Inf. Regiment Nr. 64_

Gilt nur als Quittung!   Konto-Nr.   **Sorgfältig aufbewahren!**

Der (Dienstgrad, Familienname) _Gefr. Meißner._

hat zur Überweisung an die _städt.-Sparkasse in Pasewalk._

Provinz _Pommern._ den Werthbetrag der Marken auf Seite 3 und 4 zu den folgenden Bedingungen eingezahlt:

1. Die eingezahlten Beträge sind von der Sparkasse in Reichskriegsanleihe anzulegen.

2. Die Sparkasse hat beim Eingang der ersten Einzahlung für den Einzahler ein Sparkonto anzulegen. Auf Wunsch des Einzahlers hat sie ein Sparkassenbuch auszufertigen. Von der Anlegung des Sparkontos und seiner Nummer ist der Einzahler beim Eingang der ersten Einzahlung zu benachrichtigen.

3. Die eingezahlten Beträge sind mit 5 Prozent zu verzinsen, sofern sie nicht vor Ablauf von 2 Jahren nach Friedensschluß abgehoben werden. Bei früherer Abhebung kann die Sparkasse vom Beginn der Einzahlungen an die Verzinsung auf den satzungsmäßigen Zinssatz herabsetzen.

4. Die Verzinsung beginnt mit dem Monatsersten, der auf den Tag der Einzahlung bei der Kassenverwaltung usw. folgt.

5. Sobald die eingezahlten Beträge 100 M. erreichen, hat die Sparkasse auf Wunsch des Einzahlers für je 100 M. ein Stück Kriegsanleihe zum Kurswert anzukaufen und für den Einzahler aufzubewahren. Der Ankauf gilt hinsichtlich der Verzinsung (Ziff. 3) der Abhebung gleich.

6. Im Falle des Todes des Einzahlers kann die Zahlung der Einlagen und die Herausgabe der Kriegsanleihestücke an jeden, zur gesetzlichen Hinterbliebenenversorgung Berechtigten erfolgen.

7. Lehnt die vom Einzahler angegebene Sparkasse die Annahme der Einlage ab, so wird diese einer von der Heeresverwaltung zu bestimmenden öffentlichen (Ersatz=) Sparkasse überwiesen.

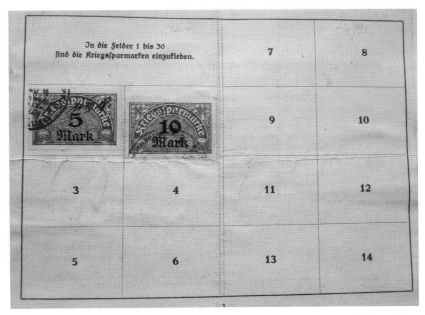

Left and above: These souvenir documents were obviously battlefield trophies removed from the pockets of a German soldier. I have not had the opportunity to have the text translated but I intend to do so and, if at all possible, I shall contact the modern relatives of the, as yet, unidentified soldier of the 64th Infantry Regiment and pass copies of the documents on. (Courtesy Pat Warren)

Contemporary handwritten note recording the arrival of the unexpected leaflet on page 105. (Courtesy Pat Warren)

11.

GERMAN WAR PROPAGANDA -
dropped by Enemy Aircraft.

Masnières near Cambrai

Sunday 27th October 1918.

scanned before being lit as firebrands for pipes and cigarettes or ignominiously tossed into the latrine boxes for later, more practical use. One bill, however, was destined for a different fate. It was thoughtfully and hopefully read by Sapper Constable, carefully folded and placed in his pack, eventually being consigned to a scrapbook with other memorabilia of the conflict. The scrapbook has remained largely unopened until now.

FLU ADDS TO CITY WOE

Devastated by over four years of unrelenting torment and anguish, the people of Coventry, as elsewhere, were dealt a further blow at the end of June, an influenza pandemic sweeping across Europe in three waves. 'At Coventry', noted the Chief Medical Officer, 'one substantial second wave reached its summit in November,' his report referring to 'one of the great historic scourges of our time, a pestilence which affected the well-being of millions of men and women and destroyed more human lives in a few months than did the European war in five years, carrying off upwards of 150,000 persons in England alone. It should be borne in mind that the fatality of the influenza is low, but its incidence is so vast that the number of deaths create an excessive mortality. It destroyed not the very young or old but the adolescent and the adult.'

A WAR TO END ALL WARS

In the House of Commons on 11 November, Lloyd George, the British Prime Minster, got to his feet and made the happiest speech of his premiership, concluding:

> 'Thus at eleven o'clock this morning came to an end the cruellest and most terrible war that has ever scourged mankind. I hope we may say that thus, this fateful morning, came to an end all wars.'

IT'S OVER!

> 'Coventry rejoiced but quietly,' noted a subdued Coventry Herald ... 'after four terrible years it is no wonder that many people have lost the ability to spontaneously rise to conditions of gaiety.'

Aftermath

The final butcher's bill for Britain and her empire was a million dead. In total, some 35,000 Coventry men enlisted during the conflict, for its size the city providing a disproportionate number of soldiers from a population that reached 136,000 in 1919.

According to Coventry's official *Roll of the Fallen* of 365 pages, published in 1927, some 2599 men died, the worst loss to one family being borne by Joseph and Eliza Bench, whose four sons, Joseph, Arthur, Ernest and Charles all perished.

The War Department spent the staggering sum of over £40.5 million in paying Coventry firms alone (Coventry citizens raised a commendable £8½ million for the war effort under the National War Savings Scheme) and it is little wonder on the day of the Armistice that Great Britain, France and Germany – three of the richest nations in the world in 1914 – were bankrupt. On top of that, Europe was indebted to its New World ally to the tune of millions of dollars and America was not willing to waive the debt any time soon.

And then those who survived came home.

A LAND NOT FIT FOR HEROES

Most men returned to Coventry exhausted and traumatized. The cheers and fanfares that had put springs in their steps in the early days of the war had long been drowned out by the thunder of guns and many returned slouching, silent and soulless. In their absence, wives had completely changed their roles, adapting to the dynamics of a convulsed world that had changed forever. Their men, whose fingers had pressed only triggers for four bloody years, needed to feel a different pulse. But they were redundant and clueless. Thousands congregated on street corners, their frustrations exploding in dramatic fashion.

Around 1.6 million woman worked in traditionally male employment during the war, 950,000 females producing over eighty per cent of the munitions. Another 100,000 worked in transport, the statistics showing a staggering increase in female employment on pre-conflict figures of 555 per cent. Womanhood was being more assertive and some ladies would soon get the vote.

Employing the charms of one well-known Coventry lady, the local authority tried to restore pre-war rhythms by arranging for the restoration of the traditional Godiva Pageant on Saturday, 18 July 1919. All went well for a while, the Mayor J. I. Bates expressing the feelings of most of the Coventry population in the following words:

'We rejoice that peace has been declared but our rejoicing is mingled with sorrow: the whole City knows that many sad hearts are amongst us. Those who have returned know the price that has been paid. Those who remained at home and waited, think of those who will never return again. Therefore the Citizens of Coventry pray that The Most High, in his infinite wisdom and compassionate memory, will, in His Own good time, heal the wounded hearts and comfort the sorrowing, May our brave dead Rest in Peace, in the name of the whole City.'

The event began with an assembly of Sunday Schools in Pool Meadow, followed by a march through the streets. But the celebrations hardly lifted the spirits, unseasonal wet weather adding to the gloom and causing the planned fireworks display to be cancelled. Simmering and pent-up animosities, fuelled by anti-German feeling centred on the King's Head Hotel, which was alleged to have had Teutonic connections, led to violence in Broadgate. Earlier on in the war, all the waiters in the hotel had been arrested as suspicious aliens and interred in a camp in Newbury. The hotel was damaged and five windows of Dunn's hat shop were smashed, a quickly summoned contingent of police officers coming under a sustained fusillade of stones, bricks and bottles, a charge with truncheons scattering the mob down Hertford Street. On the following night, the mayhem was even worse.

'Every available constable, even the office staff, was called out on duty,' commented one officer. 'Some of the people tore down the planks which were put up to guard shop windows. Women joined the mob and assisted in the hooliganism. In the Market Square, where building was in progress, granite sets had been placed in a pile. Women had filled their aprons and carried them to the leaders and threw them at anything that was capable of being smashed. Street lamps were an obvious target.'

As darkness fell on Monday, the mayhem was repeated, baton charges further dispersing an even angrier crowd. Over a hundred people were injured in the melee, a busload of police reinforcements from Birmingham arriving to be told with some pride and relief: 'We used our tools and finished the job'.

FENDING FOR YOURSELF

'At the end of World War One, there were lots of riots. Real riots. No work, factories closed down. Munitions factory closed. No dole. No social services. You had to fend for yourself. I was desperate, so I went to Arley Colliery. I couldn't be idle and I needed to help my family with the little ones that were not old enough to work. It was an endless belt. I had to stack coal on a wagon. I earned between 17 and 18 shillings a week.'

(Recollections of Arthur Keatley of Ayliffe Cottage, Fillongley. From *I Remember Strawberries & Sewage,* derived from oral recordings by Susan K More.)

TREES AND PLAQUES HONOUR THE DEAD
After an appeal in 1919, £31,562 was raised for the creation of a War Memorial Park, trees and plaques (if the bereaved could afford the not too easily raised fee of 25 shillings) marking the sacrifices of the fallen. The park was opened on 9 July 1921. A further public appeal was specifically earmarked for an imposing War Memorial in a quiet corner of the park. This was dedicated in an opening ceremony by Field Marshal Earl Haig on 8 October 1927.

DO NOT HUMILIATE GERMANY
Signed on 28 June 1919, the Treaty of Versailles ran to an exhaustive

The war memorial. (LMA)

200 pages. It punished Germany territorially and financially, J.M. Keynes, the economist, thinking that the terms were unfair. In anticipating the Armistice, American President Woodrow Wilson drew up terms for German capitulation without fully consulting his allies or even the US Congress, the onerous list of reparations drawing a guarded comment from a prescient Haig in a private conversation with his wife. The Field Marshal suggested that the allied statesmen should 'not attempt to so humiliate Germany as to produce a desire for revenge in years to come'.

I STILL REMEMBER

I began this narrative by referring to Harry Patch and it is wholly fitting that I should end with his searching comments made shortly before his death:

> 'Even ninety-two years afterwards, I still remember. I still commemorate 22 September and remember the three friends I lost on Pilckem Ridge. They are always with me. I don't do anything. I don't feel like talking. I've always remembered it. I don't join in when people sing all the old songs and I don't watch war films. Why should I? I was there. I can see that damned explosion now.'
>
> 'Why should the Government call me up and take me out to a battlefield to shoot a man I never knew, whose language I couldn't speak? All those lives lost for a war finished over a table. Now, what is the sense in that? It's just an argument between two governments. I never want any other man to go through what we did again – but still we send out lads to war, being killed and being told to kill.'

THE WAY

One who would guide a leader of men in the uses of life
will warn him against the use of arms for conquest.
Weapons often turn upon the wielder.

Where armies settle,
Nature offers nothing but briars and thorns.
After a great battle has been fought,

The land is cursed, the crops fail,
The earth lies stripped of its Motherhood.

After you have attained your purpose,
You must not parade your success,
You must not boast of your ability,
You must not feel proud;
You must rather regret that you had not been
Able to prevent war.

You must never think of conquering others by force.
Whatever strains with force
Will soon decay.
It is not attuned to the Way.
Not being attuned to the Way,
Its end comes all too soon.

Tao Te Ching
Lao Tze, 300 BC

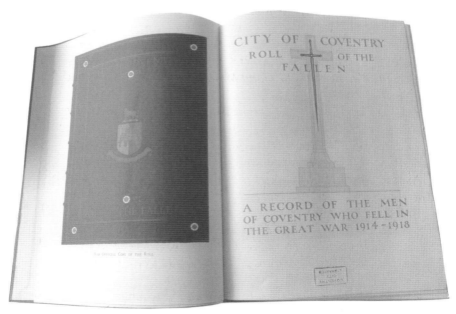

Book of Remembrance. (LMA)

Bibliography

A Strange Time – The Diary and Scrapbook of Cordelia Leigh 1914-19, Sheila Woolf and Chris Hallam, Warwickshire Great War Publications.

Earlsdon at War, Trevor Harkin, War Memorial Park Publications.

White & Poppe Ltd – Engine Manufacturers, Coventry, Jeromy Hassell, Lightmoor Press.

Bablake School and the Great War, Trevor Harkin, War Memorial Park Publications.

Pioneers to Power – The Story of the Ordinary People of Coventry, John A. Yates, The Coventry Labour Party.

The Story Behind The Monument – The 29th Division in Warwickshire and North Oxfordshire – January – March 1915, Chris Holland & Tony Jordan, Stretton Millennium History Group.

Keeping the Balance – Continuing the Story of Women in Twentieth Century Coventry, The Women's Research Group.

The Great War Letters of Roland Mountfort, Chris Holland and Rob Phillips, Matador.

Doing Its Part Nobly – Coventry's King Henry VIII School and the Great War, Chris Holland & Rob Phillips, Plott Green Publications.

Spon Street & Spon End – A detailed account of 200 years of everyday life in two of Coventry's oldest thoroughfares, John Ashby, Educational and Libraries Directorate.

The Illustrated History of Coventry's Suburbs, David McGrory, Breedon.

We Came to Coventry – memories of people from many lands who made their homes in Coventry, Coventry Reminiscence Theatre.

Bloody British History – Coventry, David McGrory, The History Press.

The Singer Story, Kevin Atkinson, Veloce Publishing.

Jubilee History 1867 - 1917 – Coventry Perseverance Co-operative Society, The Coventry Perseverance Co-operative Society.

Bushills – The Story of a Coventry Firm of Printers and Box-Makers, Ellic Howe, Thomas Bushill & Sons Ltd.

Barr's Hill School Magazine 1912-1928.

Bablake School Magazine 1911—1919.

One Soldier and Hitler, 1918. The Story of Henry Tandey VC DCM MM, David Johnson, The History Press.

I Remember Strawberries & Sewage – A Collection of Twenty Biographies, Reminiscences and Photographs of Everyday Life in the North Warwickshire Village of Fillongley, Susan K. More, Fillongley Publications.

The Townshend Chronicles – A Story of a Warwickshire Farming Family, Joy Wright, self-publication.

Pulpit & Pew – A History of Warwick Road Church 1891 – 1991, David Rimmer, Warwick Road United Reform Church.

75 Years – A record of Progress – Smiths Stamping Works Coventry, Augustus Muir, Ribble Road Works.

Still Weaving – J & J Cash Ltd of Coventry, Coventry Museum and Galleries.

Mary Dormer Harris – The Life and Work of a Warwickshire Historian, Jean Field, Brewin Books.

The Coventry and Warwickshire Hospital 1838 – 1948, Desmond Thomas Tugwood.

The Coventry We Have Lost, David Fry & Albert Smith, Simand Press.

The Character of Coventry, John Ashby.

Index